ANTONIN ARTAUD

THE PEYOTE DANCE

Translated by Helen Weaver

Artaud's experience with the Tarahumara Indians in 1936 was a psychic
ordeal and a spiritual revelation. The
images he brought back—the signs and
crosses, the movements of the peyote
dance, the ritual slaughter of the bull
and the drinking of its blood, the
echoes of Atlantis—were to haunt him
for the rest of his life. This mosaic
work, written over a period of twelve
years and spanning Artaud's stay at
the Hôpital Psychiatrique in Rodez,
documents Artaud's struggle to inte-
grate an overwhelming mystical experience into his own religious and
mental being. He writes:

"In northern Mexico there is a race
of pure red Indians called the Tarahumara. Forty thousand people are
living there in a style that predates
the flood. They are a challenge to this
world in which people talk so much
about progress only because they despair of progressing . . . I have not
come to visit the Tarahumara as a
tourist but to regain a truth which the

(*continued on back flap*)

THE PEYOTE DANCE

Antonin Artaud

*

THE
PEYOTE
DANCE

*

Translated from the French
by Helen Weaver

Farrar, Straus and Giroux
NEW YORK

Translation copyright © 1976 by Farrar, Straus and Giroux, Inc.

Artaud text © Editions Gallimard, 1971

Translated from *Les Tarahumaras, Tome IX, Oeuvres Complètes d'Antonin Artaud,* Editions Gallimard, 1971

Printed in the United States of America

Designed by Irving Perkins

Library of Congress Cataloging in Publication Data
Artaud, Antonin, 1896–1948.
The peyote dance.
Translation of Les Tarahumaras.
1. Tarahumare Indians.   2. Peyotism.   I. Title.
F1221.T25A713   1975   972'.1'00497   75–26919

Contents

✳

The Race of Lost Men   3

A Primeval Race   7

A Voyage to the Land of the Tarahumara   12
THE MOUNTAIN OF SIGNS

The Peyote Rite among the Tarahumara   18

Post-script   43

The Peyote Dance   45

The Land of the Magi Kings   59

The Rite of the Kings of Atlantis   64

Supplement to a Voyage to the Land
of the Tarahumara   70

Appendix   81

A Note on Peyote   82

Letters concerning the Tarahumara   84

Tutuguri: The Rite of Black Night   100

THE PEYOTE DANCE

*

The Race of Lost Men

*

IN NORTHERN MEXICO, forty-eight hours from Mexico City, there is a race of pure red Indians called the Tarahumara. Forty thousand people are living there in a style that predates the Flood. They are a challenge to this world in which people talk so much about progress only because they despair of progressing.

This race, which ought to be physically degenerate, has for four hundred years resisted every force that has come to attack it: civilization, interbreeding, war, winter, animals, storms, and the forest. The Tarahumara live naked in the winter in mountains that are made impassable by snow, in defiance of all medical theories. Communism exists among them in a feeling of spontaneous solidarity.

Incredible as it may seem, the Tarahumara Indians live as if they were already dead. They do not see reality and they draw magical powers from the contempt they have for civilization.

Sometimes they come to the cities, impelled by I know not what desire to move, to see, as they say, *how it is with those who are mistaken.* For them, to live in the city is to be mistaken.

3

They come with wives and children, making impossible journeys which no animal would try to attempt.

To watch them unswervingly follow their course, through torrents, ground that gives way, dense undergrowth, rock ladders, sheer walls, I cannot help thinking that they have somehow retained the instinctive force of gravitation of the first men.

✻

On first encounter, the region of the Tarahumara appears inaccessible. At best, a few poorly marked trails that every twenty yards seem to disappear under the ground. When night falls one must stop, unless one is a red man, for only a red man can see where to put his feet. When the Tarahumara come down into the cities, they beg. In a striking manner: they stop by the doors of houses and turn their heads to the side with an air of sovereign contempt. They seem to be saying: "Since you are rich, you are a dog, I am better than you, I spit on you."

Whether they are given anything or not, they always leave after the same period of time. If they are given something, they do not say thank you. For in their eyes to give to someone who has nothing is not even a duty; it is a law of physical reciprocity which the White World has betrayed. Their attitude seems to say: "In obeying the law, it is yourself you are helping, so I do not have to thank you."

The money obtained by begging is used to buy food for the return trip, for in the Tarahumara forest it is hard to see what might be the use of money.

This law of physical reciprocity which we call charity the Indians observe naturally, and without a trace of pity. Those who have nothing because they lost their harvest, because their corn has burned, because their father left them nothing, or for whatever reason which they have no need to explain, arrive at dawn at the houses of those who have something. Immediately the mistress of the house brings them whatever she has. No one looks at anyone, neither the one who gives nor the one who receives. After he has eaten, the beggar leaves without thanking or looking at anyone.

The whole life of the Tarahumara revolves around the erotic Peyote rite.

The root of the Peyote plant is hermaphroditic. It has, as we know, the shape of the male and female sexual organs combined. It is in this rite that the whole secret of these savage Indians resides. To me, its force seemed to be symbolized by the rasping stick, a piece of curved wood covered with notches which, for whole nights, the Peyote sorcerers rhythmically scrape with little sticks. But the strangest part is the way in which these sorcerers are recruited. One day, an Indian will feel *called* to handle the rasp. He goes to a sacred hiding place in the mountains, where for thousands of years there has lain an incredible collection of rasps which other sorcerers have buried. They are made of wood, the wood of warm soil, it is said. The Tarahumara will spend three years living on this plantation of rasps and, at the end of the third year, he returns—the possessor of the essential rite.

Such is the life of this strange people over whom no civilization will ever gain control.

✳

A Primeval Race

✳

To VISIT the Tarahumara is to enter a world which is incredibly anachronistic and exists in defiance of this age. As far as I am concerned, this is so much the worse for this age. So it is that the Tarahumara call themselves, feel themselves, believe themselves to be a Primeval Race, and they prove this to be true in every possible way. A Primeval Race: today no one remembers what this is, and if I had not seen the Tarahumara, I might well have believed that the expression contains a Myth. But in the Tarahumara Sierra many of the Great Ancient Myths come back to life.

The Tarahumara do not believe in God and the word "God" does not exist in their language; but they worship a transcendent principle of Nature which is Male and Female, *as it should be*. And they wear this principle on their heads like Pharaoh Initiates. Yes, this headband with two points which they use to encircle their hair indicates that they still have in their blood the consciousness of a high natural selection; that they feel themselves to be, and that they are, a race connected to those forces, originally both Male and Female, with which Nature did her creative work.

7

Similarly, Chinese who are initiated into the true traditions of their fathers also wear two braids down their backs. And Moses, in his stone statues, has two horns protruding from his forehead, one for the male on the right side, the other for the female on the left; some Tarahumara also wear their hair pulled back like horns. And this recalls, along with the statues of Moses, certain Maya or Totonac statues which have two points or two holes on the forehead, but placed one above the other, like the vestiges of an ocular system that has petrified.

Many Tarahumara Indians, whether because they do not wish to discuss it or because they have forgotten what it means, claim that this arrangement is the result of chance, and that they use the headband simply to hold their hair in place. But I have seen Tarahumara sewing headbands so that the points would hang down; and most importantly, I have seen the Peyote priests at the moment they perform this rite, which is by nature male and female, throw their European hats on the ground and put on the two-pointed headband, as if they wanted to show by this gesture that they were entering the circle of Nature with its two magnetic poles.

There is an undeniable initiation in this race; he who is close to the forces of nature participates in its secrets. But this initiation cuts both ways, so to speak. For if the Tarahumara are physically strong like Nature, it is not because they live close to Nature in a material sense, it is because they are made of the same substance as Nature and because, like all authentic manifestations of Nature, they are born of an original blend.

One might say that it is the natural Unconscious which

not only repairs in them the damages of fatigue but also corrects those natural perversions of a great principle by which they explain the existence of all infirmities. On the one hand, they show their initiation by the signs which they scatter in haunting profusion on the trees and the rocks, and on the other hand they reveal it by their physical strength, their admirable resistance to fatigue, their contempt for physical pain, injury, or illness.

It is false to say that the Tarahumara have no civilization, when we have reduced civilization to mere physical conveniences, to material commodities which the Tarahumara race has always despised.

For although the Tarahumara do not know how to work metals, although they are still at the stage of pikes and arrows, although they plow with carved tree trunks and sleep on the ground fully clothed, they have the highest idea of the philosophical movement of Nature. And they have managed to capture the secrets of this movement in their idea of Primal Numbers as successfully as Pythagoras did. The truth is that the Tarahumara despise the life of their bodies, and live only for their ideas—that is, in a constant and quasi-magical communication with the superior life of these ideas.

Each Tarahumara village is preceded by a cross, and surrounded by crosses at the four cardinal points of the mountain. It is not the cross of Christ, the Catholic cross, it is the cross of Man quartered in space, Man with his arms extended to the sides, invisible, nailed to the four cardinal points. In this the Tarahumara manifest an active geometric idea of the world to which even the human body is related.

This means: Here geometric space is alive, it has produced the best there is, that is, Man.

The stone which each Tarahumara must, under pain of
death, place at the foot of the cross when he passes is not
a superstition but a technique of awareness.

This means: Mark the point. Take note. Be aware of the
contrary forces of life, for without this awareness you are
dead.

But the Tarahumara do not fear physical death: the
body, they say, is made to disappear; it is spiritual death
that they dread, but they do not dread it in a Catholic
sense, although the Jesuits have passed their way.

There exists among the Tarahumara Indians the tradition of metempsychosis; and it is the loss of their Double
which they dread above all. Not to be aware of what one's
Double is, is to risk losing it. It is to risk a kind of abstract
fall, beyond physical space, a wandering through the high
planetary regions of the disembodied human principle.

Evil, for them, is not sin. To the Tarahumara, there is
no sin: evil is loss of consciousness. The high philosophical problems are more important to the Tarahumara than
the precepts of our Western morality.

For the Tarahumara are obsessed with philosophy; and
they are obsessed to the point of a kind of physiological
magic; with them there is no such thing as a wasted gesture, a gesture that does not have an immediate philosophical meaning. The Tarahumara become philosophers in
exactly the way a small child grows up and becomes a
man; they are philosophers by birth.

And the headband with its two points down the back
signifies that they are of a race that was originally Male

and Female; but this headband has another meaning: a
historic meaning which is obvious. The *Pouranas* carry
the memory of a war which the Male and Female principles
in Nature waged, and human beings took part in this war
between the forces of the two opposing principles. The
partisans of the natural Male principle wore white, those
of the Female principle wore red; and it was from this
esoteric and sacred red that the Phoenicians, of Female
race, derived the idea of the purple which they later com-
mercialized.

If the Tarahumara wear headbands which are sometimes white and sometimes red, it is not to affirm the
duality of the two contrary forces, but to indicate that
within the Tarahumara race the Male and Female principles of Nature exist simultaneously, and that the Tarahumara have the benefit of their combined forces. In short,
they wear their philosophy on their heads, and this philosophy reconciles the influence of the two contrary forces
in an equilibrium that partakes of the divine.

*

A Voyage to the Land
of the Tarahumara

*

THE MOUNTAIN OF SIGNS

THE LAND of the Tarahumara is full of signs, forms, and
natural effigies which in no way seem the result of chance
—as if the gods themselves, whom one feels everywhere
here, had chosen to express their powers by means of these
strange signatures in which the figure of man is hunted
down from all sides.

Of course, there are places on the earth where Nature,
moved by a kind of intelligent whim, has sculptured human forms. But here the case is different, for it is over
the whole *geographic expanse of a race* that Nature *has
chosen to speak.*

And the strange thing is that those who travel through
this region, as if seized by an unconscious paralysis, close
their senses in order to remain ignorant of everything.
When Nature, by a strange whim, suddenly shows the body
of a man being tortured on a rock, one can think at first
that this is merely a whim and that this whim signifies
nothing. But when in the course of many days on horse-

back the same intelligent charm is repeated, and *when Nature obstinately manifests the same idea;* when the same pathetic forms recur; when the heads of familiar gods appear on the rocks, and when a theme of death emanates from them, a death for which man obstinately bears the expense—when the dismembered form of man is answered by the forms of the gods who have always tortured him, *become less obscure,* more separate from a petrifying matter—when a whole area of the earth develops a philosophy parallel to that of its inhabitants; when one knows that the first men utilized a language of signs, and when one finds this language formidably expanded on the rocks, then surely one cannot continue to think that this is a whim, and that this whim signifies nothing.

If the greater part of the Tarahumara race is indigenous, and if, as they claim, they fell out of the sky into the Sierra, one may say that they fell into a *Nature that was already prepared.* And this Nature chose to think like a man. Just as she *evolved* men, she also *evolved* rocks.

This naked man who was being tortured, I saw him nailed to a rock and worked on by forms which the sun made volatile; but by I know not what optical miracle the man up there remained whole, although he was in the same light as they.

Between the mountain and myself I cannot say which was haunted, but in my voyage across the mountain I saw an optical miracle of this kind occur at least once a day.

I may have been born with a tormented body—as much a fake as the immense mountain, but a body whose obsessions are useful—and I noticed in the mountain that it is useful to have *the obsession of counting*. There was not a shadow that I did not count, when I felt it creep around something; and it was often by adding up shadows that I found my way back to strange centers.

I saw in the mountain a naked man leaning out of a large window. His head was nothing but a huge hole, a kind of circular cavity in which the sun and moon appeared by turns, according to the time of day. His right arm was stretched out like a bar but drowned in shadows and bent backward.

You could count his ribs, which numbered seven on each side. In place of the navel glittered a shiny triangle, made of what? I could not possibly say. As if Nature had chosen this piece of the mountain to expose her buried silica.

And although his head was empty, the indentations in the rock all around him gave him a precise expression in which the light made subtle changes as it advanced.

This right arm stretched forward and edged by a ray of light did not indicate an ordinary direction . . . and I was looking for what he was announcing!

It was not quite noon when I came upon this vision; I was on horseback and I was moving quickly. However, I was able to observe that what I was seeing was not sculptured forms but a certain phenomenon of light which was *superimposed* on the relief pattern of the rocks.

This figure was known to the Indians; it seemed to me by its composition and structure to obey the same principle that underlay the whole of this mountain of truncated forms. In the line of the arm there was a village surrounded by a girdle of rocks.

And I saw that the rocks all had the shape of a woman's bosom with two perfectly delineated breasts.

I saw repeated eight times the same rock which projected two shadows on the ground; I saw twice the same animal's head carrying in its jaws its effigy which it devoured; I saw, dominating the village, a kind of enormous phallic tooth with three stones at its summit and four holes on its outer face; and from their beginning, I saw all these shapes pass gradually into reality.

I seemed to read everywhere a story of childbirth in war, a story of genesis and chaos, with all these bodies of gods which were carved out like people; and these truncated statues of human forms. Not one shape which was intact, not one body which did not look as if it had emerged from a recent massacre, not one group in which I was not forced to read the struggle that divided it.

I discovered drowned men, half eaten away by the stone, and on rocks above them, other men who were struggling to keep them down. Elsewhere, an enormous statue of Death held an infant in its hand.

There is in the Cabala a music of Numbers, and this music, which reduces the chaos of the material world to its principles, explains by a kind of awesome mathematics how Nature is ordered and how she directs the birth of the forms that she pulls out of chaos. And everything I saw seemed to correspond to a number. The statues, the forms, the shadows always presented the recurring numbers 3, 4, 7, 8. The broken-off busts of women numbered 8; the phallic tooth, as I said, had three stones and four holes; the forms that became volatile numbered 12, etc. I repeat, if someone says that these forms are natural, I shall not argue; it is their repetition which is not natural. And what is even less natural is that the forms of the landscape are repeated by the Tarahumara in their rites and their dances. And these dances are not the result of chance but obey the same secret mathematics, the same concern for the subtle relations of Numbers which governs the entire Sierra region.

This inhabited Sierra, this Sierra which exhales a metaphysical thinking in its rocks, the Tarahumara have covered with signs, signs that are completely conscious, intelligent, and purposeful.

At every bend in the road one sees trees that have *deliberately* been burned in the shape of a cross, or in the shape of creatures, and often these creatures are double and face each other, as if to manifest the essential *duality* of things; and I have seen this duality reduced to its principle in a sign in the shape *ʄ/* surrounded by a circle, which I saw branded with a red-hot iron on a tall pine; other trees bore spears, trefoils, or acanthus leaves surrounded by crosses; here and there, in places with steep embankments, narrow passageways between rocks, lines of Egyptian anserated crosses grew into processions; and the doors of the Tarahumara houses displayed the sign of the Mayan world: two facing triangles with their points connected by a bar; and this bar is the Tree of Life which passes through the center of Reality.

As I travel through the mountain, these spears, these crosses, these trefoils, these leafy hearts, these composite crosses, these triangles, these creatures facing each other and opposing each other to mark their eternal conflict, their division, their duality, awaken strange memories in me. I remember suddenly that there were, in History, Sects which inlaid these same signs upon rocks, carved out of jade, beaten into iron, or chiseled. And I begin to think that this symbolism conceals a Science. And I find it strange that the primitive people of the Tarahumara tribe, whose rites and culture are older than the Flood, actually possessed this science well before the appearance of the Legend of the Grail, or the founding of the Sect of the Rosicrucians.

The Peyote Rite among
the Tarahumara

*

It was the priests of Tutuguri who showed me the way of
Ciguri, just as a few days earlier the *Master of All Things*
had shown me the way of Tutuguri. The *Master of All
Things* governs external relations between people: friend-
ship, pity, charity, loyalty, piety, generosity, work. His
power stops at the threshold of what is known in Europe
as metaphysics or theology, but it goes much further into
the realm of inner consciousness than that of any European political leader. In Mexico no one can be initiated,
that is, receive the unction of the priests of the Sun and
the immersive and reinstating blow of the priests of Ciguri, which is a rite of humiliation, unless he has previ-
ously been touched by the sword of the old Indian chief
who has authority over peace and war, over Justice, Mar-
riage, and Love. He seems to have control over those forces
which compel people to love each other or which drive
them mad, whereas the priests of Tutuguri invoke with
their mouths that Spirit which creates men and places
them in the Infinite from which the Soul must collect them
and rearrange them in its self. The influence of the priests

of the Sun surrounds the whole soul and stops at the had shown me the way of Tutuguri. The *Master of All Things* picks up the reverberation. And it was at this boundary that the old Mexican chief struck me in order to reawaken my consciousness, for to understand the Sun I was not well born; for the hierarchical order of things dictates that, after passing through the ALL, that is the many, which is matter, one returns to the simplicity of the one, which is Tutuguri or the Sun, only to dissolve and be reborn by means of this process of mysterious reassimilation. This dark reassimilation is contained within Ciguri, as a Myth of reawakening, then of destruction, and finally of resolution in the sieve of supreme surrender, as their priests are incessantly shouting and affirming in their Dance of All the Night. For it lasts the entire night, from sunset to dawn, but it takes the whole night and gathers it as one gathers all the juice of a fruit at the very source of life. And the eradication of ownership extends to god and even beyond; for not even god, least of all god, can take that part of the self which is authentically one's own, however foolishly it may be abandoned.

It was on a Sunday morning that the old Indian chief awakened my consciousness with a prick of the sword between the spleen and the heart. "Have confidence," he said to me, "have no fear, I will do you no harm," and he quickly retreated three or four steps and, after describing a circle in the air behind him with his sword, rushed forward and leaped at me with all his strength, as if he meant to destroy me. But the point of his sword barely grazed my skin and drew only a tiny drop of blood. I felt no pain whatsoever, but I did have the impression of awakening

to something for which until then I had been ill endowed
and ill prepared, and I felt filled with a light which I had
never before possessed. It was a few days later that one
morning at dawn I entered into relation with the priests
of Tutuguri and two days after that that I finally made
contact with Ciguri.

"To sew you back together in your wholeness, without
God who assimilates you and creates you, as if you were
creating yourself, and as you yourself create yourself out
of Nothingness and in spite of Him at every moment."

These are the very words of the Indian chief and I am
merely reporting them, not as he said them to me, but as
I have *reconstructed* them under the fantastic illuminations of Ciguri.

Now if the Priests of the Sun behave like manifestations
of the Word of God, or of his Logos, that is, Jesus Christ,
the Priests of Peyote allowed me to experience the actual
Myth of the Mystery, to become immersed in the original
mythic arcana, to enter through them into the Mystery of
Mysteries, to look upon the face of those extreme opera-
tions by which THE FATHER MAN, NEITHER MAN NOR
WOMAN, created all things. To be sure I did not catch all
this immediately and it took me a while to understand it,
and indeed, many of the dance movements, many of the
attitudes or the shapes which the priests of Ciguri draw in
the air as if they were imposing them on the darkness or
drawing them from the caves of night, they themselves
do not understand, and in performing them they are merely
obeying on the one hand a kind of physical tradition, and
on the other the secret commands issued to them by the
Peyote whose essence they absorb before they start danc-

ing, in order to achieve a trance state. I mean that they do what the plant tells them to do; they repeat it like a kind of lesson which their muscles obey, but which they no longer understand in the relaxation of their nerves, any more than their fathers or grandfathers before them. For the function of every nerve is strained. This did not satisfy me and when the Dance was over I wanted to find out more. For before witnessing the Rite of Ciguri as it is performed by living Indian priests, I had questioned many Tarahumara on the mountain and had spent the night with a young family of whom the husband was an adept of this rite and seemed to know many of its secrets. And I received from him some marvelous explanations and extremely precise elucidations of the way in which Peyote revives throughout the nervous system the memory of certain supreme truths by means of which human consciousness does not lose but on the contrary regains its perception of the Infinite. "The nature of these truths," this man told me, "it is not my business to show you. But it is my business to reawaken them in the mind of your human existence. The mind of man is tired of God, because it is bad and sick, and it is up to us to make it hungry for Him. But as you see, Time itself refuses us the means. You will be shown tomorrow what we still can do. And if you wish to work with us, perhaps with the aid of the Good Will of a man who has come from the other side of the sea and who is not of our Race, we shall succeed in breaking down one more barrier." CIGURI is a name which Indian ears do not like to hear pronounced. I had with me a *mestizo* guide who also acted as my interpreter with the Tarahumara, and he had warned me to mention it to them only with respect and caution because, he told me, *they are afraid of it.* But I observed that if there is any emotion that is alien to them in this connection it is fear, and that, on the contrary, the word awakens in them that sense of the sacred which European consciousness has lost, and this is the root of all our misfortunes, for here people no longer respect anything. And the series of attitudes the young Indian assumed before my eyes when I uttered the word CIGURI taught me many things about the potentialities of human consciousness when it has retained the sense of God. I will admit that a terror emanated from his gestures, but the terror was not his own, for it covered him as if with a shield or a mantle. He seemed happy as one is only in the supreme moments of existence, his face overflowing with joy and adoration. So must they have stood, the First Born of a humanity still in childbirth when the spirit of MAN UNCREATED rose in thunder and flames over the eviscerated world; so must they have prayed in the catacombs, those skeletons to whom it is written that MAN himself appeared.

He joined his hands and his eyes kindled. His face became transfixed and closed. But the more he withdrew into himself, the more I had the impression that a strange and legible emotion radiated physically from him. He moved two or three times. And each time his eyes, which had become almost fixed, returned to a point next to him, as if he wanted to be aware of something that was to be feared. But I realized that what he might be afraid of was falling short of the respect he owed to God, through some sort of negligence. And I observed two very important things: the first was that the Tarahumara Indian does not attach the same value to his body that we Europeans do, and that he has an entirely different notion of it. "It isn't I at all," he seemed to say, "who am this body," and when he turned to stare at something next to him it was his body itself that he seemed to examine and observe.

"Where I am myself and what I am, it is Ciguri who tells it to me and dictates it to me, and you who lie and disobey. What I feel in reality you are never willing to feel, and you give me contrary sensations. You want nothing of what I want. And what you propose to me most of the time is Evil. You have been nothing but a transitory ordeal and a burden. Someday I shall command you to leave when *Ciguri* himself will be free, but," he said suddenly, weeping, "you must not leave altogether. *It was Ciguri*, after all, who made you and many times you have provided me with a refuge from the storm, *for Ciguri would die if he did not have me.*"

The second thing I observed in the middle of this prayer —for this series of movements in front of himself and as if beside himself which I had just witnessed, and which took much less time to perform than I have taken to report it, constituted the Indian's impromptu prayer at the mere sound of the name *Ciguri*—the second thing that struck me is that if the Indian is the enemy of his body, he seems also to have sacrificed his consciousness to God, and it seems that the habit of Peyote guides him in this work. The emotions which radiated from him, which passed across his face one after the other, and which could be read, *were manifestly not his own;* he did not attribute them to himself, he no longer identified with what for us is a personal emotion, or rather he did not do it in our way, as the result of a choice and of an instant flashing incubation as we do. Among all the ideas that pass through our heads there are those we accept and those we do not accept. On the day when our self and our consciousness are formed there is established within this incessant movement of incubation a distinctive rhythm and a natural choice whereby only our own ideas remain in the field of consciousness, and the rest automatically vanish. It may take us time to carve out of our emotions and isolate from them our own face, but the way we think on the most important points is like the *totem* of an indisputable grammar that measures its terms word for word. And our self, when we question it, always responds in the same way: like someone who knows that it is he who answers and not another. It is not like this with the Indian.

A European would never allow himself to think that something he has felt and perceived in his body, an emotion which has shaken him, a strange idea which he has just had and which has inspired him with its beauty, was not his own, and that someone else has felt and experienced all this in his own body—or else he would believe himself mad and people would probably say that he had become a lunatic. The Tarahumara, on the contrary, systematically distinguishes between what is his own and what is of the Other in everything he thinks, feels, and does. But what makes him different from a lunatic is that his personal consciousness has expanded in this process of internal separation and distribution to which Peyote has led him and which strengthens his will. Although he may seem to know what he is *not* much better than what he is, he does know what he is and who he is much better than we know

what we are and what we want. "There is," he said, "in
every man an ancient reflection of God in which we can
still contemplate the image of that infinite force which one
day flung us into a soul and this soul into a body, and it is
to the image of this Force that Peyote has led us because
Ciguri calls us back to him."

What I observed of this Indian who had not taken Peyote
for a long time, but was one of the adepts of its Rites—
for the Rite of Ciguri is the summit of the religion of the
Tarahumara—instilled in me the greatest desire to see all
these Rites myself *and to obtain permission to participate
in them.* That was the difficult part.

The friendliness shown me by this young Tarahumara
who was not afraid to start praying a few feet away from
me was already a guarantee that certain doors would be
opened. Moreover, what he had said about the help that
was expected from me made me think that my admission
to the Rites of *Ciguri* depended partly on what I could do
to overcome the resistance the Tarahumara were encoun-
tering from the *mestizo* government of Mexico to the observance of their Rites. Although *mestizo,* this government
is pro-Indian because those who hold office have more
red blood than white. But the distribution is not propor-
tionate, and government representatives in the mountains
are almost wholly of mixed blood. And they regard the
beliefs of the Old Mexicans as dangerous. The present
government of Mexico has founded native schools in the
mountains where Indian children are given an instruction
patterned after that of French elementary schools, and the
head of the Department of Public Education of Mexico,
from whom the French ambassador had obtained a permit

for me, gave me lodgings in the native school of the Tara-humara. Thus I had made the acquaintance of the director of this school, who was also in charge of discipline through-out the Tarahumara territory, and who had under him a division of cavalry. Although no steps had yet been taken in the matter, I knew that the official intention was to pro-hibit the next Peyote celebration, which was to take place in a few days. In addition to the great Racial Festival in which all the Tarahumara participate and which takes place at a fixed date, like our Christmas, the Tarahumara also have a number of special Rites based on Peyote. And they had consented to show me one of these. In the reli-gion of the Tarahumara there are other holidays, just as here we have Easter, the Feast of the Ascension, the Feast of the Assumption, and the Feast of the Immaculate Con-ception, but they do not all involve Peyote, and the Great Feast of *Ciguri* takes place, I believe, only once a year. It is then that it is taken according to all the age-old tradi-tional rites. Peyote is also taken on the other holidays but only as an occasional adjuvant and with no attention to graduating its force or effects. When I say that Peyote is taken I ought rather to say that it *was* taken, because the Mexican government is doing everything in its power to take Peyote away from the Tarahumara and to prevent their coming under its influence, and soldiers sent by the government into the mountains have received orders to prevent its cultivation. On my arrival in the mountains I found the Tarahumara desperate because of the recent destruction of a field of Peyote by the soldiers of Mexico City.

I had a long conversation on this subject with the director

of the native school where I stayed. This conversation was heated, difficult, and sometimes repugnant. The mestizo director of the Tarahumara native school was much more preoccupied with his sex, which enabled him each night to possess the schoolmistress, a mestizo like himself, than with culture or religion. But the government of Mexico had based its program on a return to Indian culture and in spite of everything the man was reluctant to shed Indian blood.

"CIGURI," I told him, "is not a plant, it is a man whom you have castrated by blowing up the Peyote field. And for this red and mutilated member which sings—green, white, lilac—the people want to call you to account. And they see it." I noticed as I passed through several Tarahumara villages that a wind of revolt was blowing over the tribe at the appearance of the red member. The director of the native school was not unaware of this, but he was undecided about what method to use to restore calm among the Indians. "The only method," I told him, "is to succeed in winning their hearts. They will never forgive you for this destruction, but you can show them by an opposite action that you are not an enemy of God. You are only a handful here and if they decided to revolt you would have to make war on them, and even with your weapons you could not hold out. Besides, the Priests of Ciguri have hiding places where you will never be able to go.

"And what would become of the return of Mexico to Indian culture in the face of civil war? You must authorize this Festival at once if you want to have any Tarahumara left, and you must also provide the tribes with facilities for gathering, so that they will feel that you are sympathetic to them."

"The trouble is that when they have taken Peyote, they no longer obey us."

"It is the same with Peyote as it is with everything human. It is a marvelous magnetic and alchemical principle, provided one knows how to take it—that is to say, in the proper doses and according to the proper gradations. And above all, provided one does not take it at the wrong time or in the wrong place. If after taking Peyote the Indians seem to go mad, it is because they are abusing it in order to reach that point of disorderly intoxication in which the soul is no longer subject to anything. In so doing, it is not you whom they are disobeying but *Ciguri* itself, for Ciguri is the God of the Prescience of the just, of equilibrium and of self-control. He who has *truly* imbibed Ciguri, the true meter and measure of Ciguri, MAN and not indeterminate PHANTOM, knows how things are made and he can no longer lose his reason, because it is God who is in his nerves and who guides them.

"But to drink Ciguri is by definition not to exceed the dose, for Ciguri is the Infinite, and the mystery of the therapeutic action of remedies is related to the proportion in which our organism takes them. To exceed what is necessary is to VIOLATE that action.

"According to the sacerdotal traditions of the Tarahumara, God disappears immediately when one has taken too much and in his place it is the Evil Spirit who comes."

"Tomorrow evening you will make the acquaintance of a family of Priests of Ciguri," said the director of the native school. "Tell them what you just told me and I am sure that this time again and perhaps more than the last few times we shall succeed in keeping the absorption of Peyote within bounds. Tell them also that this Feast will be authorized and that we will do everything in our power to make the gathering possible and that to this end we shall provide them with whatever horses and supplies they may need."

In the late afternoon of the next day I arrived at the little Indian village where I had been told that the Rite of Peyote was to be shown me. It took place after dark. The priest arrived with two assistants, a man and a woman, and two young children. He drew on the ground a kind of large semicircle inside which the revels of his assistants were to take place and he closed this semicircle with a stout beam on which I was permitted to sit. To the right, the arc of the circle was bounded by a kind of retreat in the shape of an 8 which I understood constituted for the priest the Holy of Holies. To the left, there was the Void: this is where the children stood. It was in the Holy of Holies that the old wooden pot containing the Peyote roots was placed, for the Priests do not use the whole plant for their special Rites, or at least not any more.

The Priest had a cane in his hand and the children had little sticks. Peyote is taken after a certain number of dance movements and when, by the religious performance of the Rite, its adepts have achieved a state in which Ciguri wishes to enter into them.

I observed that the assistants were having trouble starting to move, and I had the impression that they would not dance or would dance badly if they did not know that at the appropriate moment Ciguri was going to descend upon them. For the Rite of Ciguri is a Rite of creation, which explains how things *are* in the Void and how the Void is in the Infinite, and how they emerged from it into Reality, and were made. And the Rite is completed at the moment when, at God's command, the things have taken on Being in a body. This is what the two assistants danced, but this did not take place without a long discussion.

"We can no longer understand God unless he first touches our souls, and our dance will be nothing but a mockery, and the PHANTOM," they screamed, "the PHANTOM which pursues CIGURI will be born here once again."

The Priest took a long time making up his mind, but finally he drew from his breast a small bag and poured into the Indians' hands a kind of white powder which they immediately consumed.

Whereupon they began to dance. Seeing their faces after they had taken this powdered Peyote, I realized that they were going to show me something which I had never experienced before. And I gave all my attention so that I would miss nothing of what I was going to see.

The two assistants lay down on the ground facing each other like two inanimate balls. But the old Priest must have taken the powder himself, for an inhuman expression had stolen over his face. I saw him stretch and stand very tall. His eyes kindled and began to take on an expression of unusual authority. With his cane he made two or three dull thuds on the ground, then entered the 8 he had drawn to the right of the Ritual Field. Now the assistants seemed to emerge from their inanimate state. First the man shook his head and struck the ground with the palms of his hands. The woman shook her back. Then the Priest spat:

not saliva, but his breath. Noisily he expelled his breath between his teeth. Under the influence of this pulmonary vibration, the man and woman simultaneously came to life and rose to their feet. But from the way they stood facing each other, especially from the way each stood in space as they might have stood in the pockets of the void and the cracks of the infinite, it was clear that it was no longer a man and a woman who were there but two principles: the male, mouth open, gums smacking, red, flaming, bloody, as if lacerated by the roots of the teeth, which were translucent at that moment like tongues of command; the female, toothless larva, molars filed down, like a she-rat in its cage, imprisoned in her own heat, shifting and turning in front of the hirsute male; and it was also clear that they were going to collide, smash frantically into one another just as material things, after facing each other for a time and making war, finally intermingle before the *indiscreet* and *guilty* eye of God, whom their action will gradually replace. "For *Ciguri*," they say, "was MAN, MAN as SELF-CREATED, HIMSELF in the space HE *was constructing* FOR HIMSELF, when God murdered him."

This is exactly what took place.

But one thing struck me particularly in the way they threatened each other, avoided each other, collided with each other, and finally consented to unite. This is that these principles were not in the body, never reached the body, but obstinately remained like two immaterial ideas suspended outside of Being, eternally opposed to HIM, and which moreover made *their own bodies*, bodies in which the idea of matter is volatilized by CIGURI. As I watched them, I remembered everything I had been told about

Indian religion and culture by the poets, teachers, and artists of all kinds whom I knew in Mexico, and what I had read in all the books I had borrowed about the metaphysical traditions of the Mexicans.

"The Evil Spirit," say the Initiate Priests of Ciguri, "has never been able or willing to believe that God is not accessibly and exclusively a Being and that there is something more than Being in the inscrutable essence of God."

But this was exactly what this Peyote Dance was in the process of showing me.

For in this dance I thought I could see the point where the universal unconscious is sick. And that it is outside of God. The priest would touch his spleen or his liver with his right hand while with his left hand he struck the ground with his cane. Each of his gestures evoked from the man and the woman a distant attitude—now of desperate and haughty affirmation, now of enraged denial. But when the Priest, who now held his cane in both hands, struck several rapid blows, they advanced rhythmically toward each other with their elbows apart and their hands joined, so that they formed two triangles in motion. At the same time their feet drew on the ground circles, and something that resembled the limbs of a letter, an S, a U, a J, a V. Figures in which the 8 shape recurred most often. Once, twice they did not meet but passed one another with a tentative greeting. The third time their greeting became more certain. The fourth time they joined hands, circled each other, and the man's feet seemed to search on the ground for the places where the woman's feet had struck it.

They repeated this sequence eight times. But after the fourth time their faces, which had taken on a lively expression, never ceased to be radiant. The eighth time they looked toward the Priest, who then moved with a dominating and menacing air to the furthest end of the Holy of Holies, where things are in contact with the North. And with his cane he drew in the air a huge 8. But the scream that he uttered at that moment could have overthrown *the hellish labor pains of the dead man black with his ancient sin,* in the words of the old buried poem of the Maya of Yucatán; and I do not remember ever in my life hearing anything that revealed more clearly or resonantly to what depths the human will descends to raise its foreknowledge of night. And I seemed to see again in the Infinite and as if in a dream the raw matter from which God called forth Life. This scream of the Priest seemed meant to sustain the path of the cane in the air. Screaming this way, the Priest moved and he drew with his whole body in the air and with his feet on the ground the shape of the same 8 until he had closed the figure at the Southern end.

The dance was almost over. The two children who had remained to the left of the circle all this time asked whether they could go, and the Priest gave them a sign with his cane as if to scatter and disappear. But neither of the two had taken Peyote. They made a vague gesture that resembled a dance movement, then gave up and disappeared as if to go home.

As I said at the beginning of this account, all this did not satisfy me. I wanted to find out more about Peyote. I walked over to the Priest to question him.

"Our last Festival," he told me, "could not take place. We are discouraged. Nowadays we do not take Ciguri for the Rites but as a vice. Soon our whole Race will be sick. Time has grown too old for Man. It can no longer sustain us. What are we to do, what is to become of us? Already our people are turning away from God. As a priest, I cannot help feeling it. You see me in despair."

I told him about the agreement that had been made with the director of the native school and that this time their next great festival could take place.

I also told him that I had not come to visit the Tarahumara as a tourist but to regain a Truth which the world of Europe is losing and which his Race had preserved. This disarmed him completely and he told me some wonderful things about Good and Evil, about Truth and Life.

"Everything I say comes from *Ciguri*," he told me, "and it was *Ciguri* that taught it to me.

"Things are not as we see them and experience them most of the time, but they are as *Ciguri* teaches them to us. They have been taken over by Evil, by the Evil Spirit since time began, and without *Ciguri* it is impossible for man to return to the Truth. In the beginning they were true, but the older we grow the more false they become, because the more they are taken over by Evil. The world in the beginning was completely real, it resounded in the human heart and with the human heart. Now the heart is no longer in it, nor is the soul because God has withdrawn from it. To see the things of the world was to see the Infinite. Now when I look at the light I have trouble thinking of God. And yet it is He, Ciguri, who made everything. But Evil is in all things and I, as a man, can no longer feel pure. There is inside me something horrible which rises and which does not come from me, but from the shadows that I have in me, where the soul of man does not know where the *I* begins and where it ends, or what made it begin as it sees itself. And this is what *Ciguri* tells me. With *Ciguri* I no longer know untruth and I no longer confuse *that which wills* truly in every man with that which does not will but mimics being with ill will. And soon that is all there will be," he said, retreating several steps: "this obscene mask of someone sniggering between the sperm and the dung."

These words of the Priest which I have just reported are absolutely authentic; I found them too important and too beautiful to allow myself to change them in any way, and if I have not reported them word for word the difference is very slight, for you must understand that they impressed me profoundly and that my recollection on this point has remained extremely precise. As I said before, he had just taken Peyote and I was not surprised at his lucidity.

When this conversation was over he asked me whether I would like to taste Ciguri myself and in this way to come closer to the Truth I was seeking.

I told him that this was my fondest desire and that I did not think that without the help of Peyote one could reach everything which eludes us and from which we are becoming more and more alienated by time and material things.

Into my left hand he poured a quantity the size of a ripe almond, "enough," he said, "to see God two or three times, for God can never be known. To enter into his presence one must come under the influence of Ciguri at least three times, but each dose must not exceed the size of a pea."

So I spent another day or two among the Tarahumara to deepen my experience of Peyote, and it would require a large volume to report everything I saw and felt under its influence and everything that the priests, their assistants, and their families told me on the subject. But a vision which I had and which impressed me was declared *authentic* by the Priest and his family; it concerned, apparently, the one who must be *Ciguri* and who is God. But one arrives at such a vision only after one has gone through a tearing and an agony, after which one feels as if turned around and *reversed* to the other side of things, and one no longer understands the world that one has just left.

I said *reversed* to the other side of things, as if a terrible force had granted that you be *restored* to that which exists on the other side. You no longer feel the body which you have just left and which secured you within its limits, but you feel much happier to belong to the limitless than to yourself, for you understand that what was yourself has come from the head of this limitless, the Infinite, and that you are going to see it. You feel as if you were in an effervescent wave which gives off an incessant crackling in all directions. Things which seem to have emerged from what was your spleen, your liver, your heart, or your lungs keep breaking away and bursting in this atmosphere which wavers between gas and water, but which seems to summon forth material things and command them to combine.

The things that emerged from my spleen or my liver were shaped like the letters of a very ancient and mysterious alphabet chewed by an enormous mouth, but terrify-

ingly obscure, proud, *illegible,* jealous of its invisibility;
and these signs were swept in all directions in space while
I seemed to ascend, but not alone. Aided by a strange
force. But much freer than when on the earth I was alone.
At a given moment something like a wind arose and
space shrank back. On the side where my spleen was, an
immense void was hollowed out which was painted gray
and pink like the shore of the sea. And at the bottom of
this void there appeared the form of a stranded root, a kind
of J that had at its summit three branches surmounted by
an E that was as sad and luminous as an eye. Flames
came out of the left ear of the J and, passing behind it,
seemed to push all things to the right, to the side where
my liver was, but far beyond it. I saw no more and everything vanished or it was I who vanished as I returned to
ordinary reality. In any case, it seems that I had seen the
very Spirit of Ciguri. And I believe that this must have
objectively corresponded to a *painted* transcendental rep-
resentation of the ultimate and highest realities; and the
Mystics must go through similar states and images before
they reach, according to the formula, the supreme burn-
ings and rendings after which they fall beneath the kiss
of God like whores, no doubt, into the arms of their pro-
curers.

This experience inspired a number of reflections on the
psychic effects of Peyote.*

---

* I mean that although these mystical ideas may once again im-
pose themselves on my thinking, Peyote, on the other hand, does not
lend itself to these fetid spiritual assimilations, for MYSTICISM has
never been anything but the copulation of a very learned and refined
hypocrisy against which PEYOTE as a whole protests, for with Peyote

Peyote leads the self back to its true sources. Once one has experienced a visionary state of this kind, one can no longer confuse the lie with the truth. One has seen where one comes from and who one is, and one no longer doubts what one is. There is no emotion or external influence that can divert one from this reality.

And the whole series of lustful fantasies projected by the unconscious can no longer oppress the true breath of MAN, for the good reason that Peyote is MAN not born, but INBORN, and that with it the atavistic and personal consciousness is summoned and supported. It knows what is good for it and what is of no use to it: it knows which thoughts and feelings it can receive without danger and *with profit*, and which are harmful to the exercise of its freedom. Above all, it knows just how far its own being goes, and just how far *it has not yet gone* OR HAS NOT THE RIGHT TO GO WITHOUT SINKING INTO THE UNREAL, THE ILLUSORY, THE UNMADE, THE UNPREPARED.

To take one's dreams for realities (a state into which Peyote will never let you sink) is where one might confuse perceptions taken from the depths—fleeting, uncultivated, not yet ripe, not yet arisen from the hallucinatory unconscious—with the images and emotions of the real. For there is in consciousness a *Magic* with which one can go beyond things. And Peyote tells us where this Magic is, and after what strange concretions, whose breath is

---

MAN is alone, desperately scraping out the music of his own skeleton, without father, mother, family, love, god, or society.

And no living being to accompany him. And the skeleton is not of bone but of skin, like a skin that walks. And one walks from the equinox to the solstice, buckling on one's own humanity. [Note added by Artaud in 1947.]

atavistically compressed and obstructed, the Fantastic can emerge and can once again scatter in our consciousness its phosphorescence and its haze. And this Fantastic is of noble quality, its disorder is only apparent, it really obeys an order that is fashioned mysteriously and on a level which normal consciousness does not reach but which *Ciguri* allows us to reach, and which is the very mystery of all poetry. But there is in human existence another level, obscure and formless, where consciousness has not entered, and which surrounds it like a mysterious extension or a menace, as the case may be. And which itself gives off adventurous sensations, perceptions. These are those shameless fantasies which affect an unhealthy mind, which abandons itself to them and dissolves in them completely if it finds nothing to hold it back. And Peyote is the only barrier that Evil encounters on this terrible frontier.

I too have had false sensations and perceptions and I have believed in them. In June, July, August, and early September last year I believed that I was surrounded by demons, and I thought I could feel them, could see them taking shape around me. The only way I could drive them away was to keep making the sign of the cross over every point on my body or in space where I thought I saw them. I would also write on any scrap of paper or book within reach, incantations which were not worth much either from a literary point of view or as magic, for things written in this state are no more than the residue, the distortion, or rather the *counterfeit* of the high illuminations of LIFE. By the end of last September these bad ideas, these false ideas, these obsessive and inherently worthless perceptions began to disappear; by October they were virtually

gone. Around the 15th or 20th of last November I felt my
energy and my lucidity coming back. Above all, I felt that
my mind was finally clear. No more erroneous sensations.
No more bad perceptions. Now with every day a sense of
security, of inner certainty, is slowly but surely growing
within me.

If I have recently made gestures which resemble those
of certain victims of *religious mania*, they are merely the
residue of the regrettable habits I adopted because of beliefs which did not exist. As the sea when it withdraws
leaves on the sand a varied deposit which the wind sweeps
away, I have for several weeks concentrated all my will
power on ridding myself of these little remnants. And I
observe that they are gradually disappearing.

There is one thing which the Peyote priests of Mexico
helped me to notice, and which the small amount of Peyote
I took brought to my consciousness. This is that in the
human liver there occurs that secret alchemy and that
process by which the self of each individual chooses what
suits it from among the sensations, emotions, and desires
which the unconscious shapes and which make up its appetites, its conceptions, its true beliefs, and its *ideas*. It is
here that the I becomes conscious and that its power of
deliberation, of extreme organic discrimination, is de-
ployed. Because it is here that *Ciguri* works to separate
what exists from what does not exist. The liver seems,
therefore, to be the organic filter of the *Unconscious*.

I have found similar metaphysical ideas in the works of
the ancient Chinese. According to them the liver is the
filter of the unconscious but the spleen is the physical
counterpart of the infinite. But that is another matter.

But in order for the liver to perform its function it is necessary at least that the body be well nourished.

One cannot reproach a man who has been shut up in an insane asylum for six years and who for three years has not had enough to eat for some *mysterious* weakening of the Will. I sometimes go for months without eating a piece of sugar or chocolate. As for butter, I have forgotten how long it has been since I tasted it.

I never get up from the table without a feeling of hunger because rations, as you know, are greatly reduced. *And, above all, there is not enough bread.* Before the piece of chocolate which was given to me the day before yesterday, Friday, I had not eaten chocolate for eight months. I am not a man who allows himself to be diverted from doing his duty by anything, but at least let me not be reproached for lack of energy in times like these, when those elements which arc necessary to the renewal of energy no longer exist in the nourishment we receive. And, above all, let me not be subjected to more electric-shock treatments for lapses which it is well known are not beyond the control of my own will, lucidity, and intelligence. Enough, enough, and more than enough of this trauma of punishment.

Each electric-shock treatment plunged me into a terror which always lasted several hours. And I could not face each new treatment without despair, for I knew that once again I would lose consciousness and that for one whole day I would be gasping for air inside myself, unable to find myself, knowing perfectly well that I was somewhere but the devil knew where, as if I were *dead.*

All this has taken us far from healing by Peyote. According to what I saw, Peyote *fixes* the mind and prevents it from wandering, from surrendering to false impressions. The Mexican Priests showed me the exact point on the liver where *Ciguri* or Peyote produces this synthetic concretion which maintains permanently in the mind a sense of and a desire for the real and gives it the strength to surrender to that while automatically rejecting the rest.

"It is like the skeleton leader who returns," the Tarahumara said of that DARK RITE, "THE NIGHT WHICH MARCHES ON THE NIGHT."

Post-script

The Peyote Rite was written in Rodez during the first year of my arrival at the asylum, after I had already been shut up for seven years, three of them in solitary confinement, with systematic and daily poisoning. It represents my first effort to return to myself after seven years of estrangement and total castration. In it a recent victim of poisoning, sequestered and traumatized, recalls what happened before his death. This explains why the text can do no more than stammer. I should add that it was written in the dulled mental state of a *convert* whom the magical spells of the priestly rabble, taking advantage of his momentary weakness, were keeping in a state of enslavement.

Ivry-sur-Seine, March 10, 1947

I wrote *The Peyote Rite* in a state of conversion, and with at least one hundred and fifty to two hundred recent hosts in my body,

whence my delirium here and there on the subject of Christ, and the cross of Jesus Christ.

For nothing now appears to me more funereal or more

mortally disastrous than the stratifying and limited sign of
the cross,

nothing more erotically pornographic than Christ, ig-
noble sexual materialization of all the false psychic enig-
mas, all the bodily wastes that have been passed to the
intelligence because they have nothing more to do in the
world than to serve as matter for riddles, and whose basest
maneuvers of magical masturbation trigger an electric re-
lease from prison.

Paris, March 23, 1947

*

The Peyote Dance

*

THE PHYSICAL HOLD was still there. This cataclysm which
was my body . . . After twenty-eight days of waiting, I had
not yet come back into myself or, I should say, *gone out*
into myself. Into myself, into this dislocated assemblage,
this piece of damaged geology.

Inert, as earth with its rocks can be—and all those crev-
ices that run in sedimentary layers piled on top of each
other. Friable, of course, I was—not in places, but as a
whole—from my first moment of contact with this terrible
mountain which I am sure had raised barriers against me
to prevent me from entering. And since I've been up there,
the supernatural no longer seems to me something so extraordinary that I cannot say that I was, in the literal sense
of the word, *bewitched*.

To take a step was for me no longer to take a step; but
to feel *where* I was carrying my head. Can you understand
this? Limbs which obey one after the other, and which one
moves forward one after the other; and the vertical position above the earth which must be maintained. For the
head, overflowing with waves, the head which can no longer
control its whirling, the head feels all the whirling energies

of the earth below, which bewilder it and keep it from remaining erect.

Twenty-eight days of this heavy captivity, this ill-assem-
bled heap of organs which I was and which I had the impression of witnessing like a vast landscape of ice on the
point of breaking up.

The hold was therefore upon me, so terrible that to go
from the house of the Indian to a tree located a few steps
away required more than courage, required summoning the
reserve forces of a truly *desperate* will. For to have come
this far, to find myself at last on the threshold of an encounter and of this place from which I expected so many
revelations, and to feel so lost, so abandoned, so deposed.
Had I ever known joy, had there ever in the world been a
sensation which was not one of anguish or of irremissible
despair; had I ever been in a state other than that intersti-
tial pain which every night pursued me? Was there anything for me which was not at the gate of death, and could
at least one body be found, a single human body which
escaped my perpetual crucifixion?

It required, of course, an act of the will for me to believe
that something was going to happen. And all this, for what?
For a dance, for a rite of lost Indians who no longer even
know who they are or where they come from and who,
when you question them, answer with tales whose connection and secret they have lost.

After an exhaustion so cruel, I repeat, that I can no
longer believe that I was not in fact bewitched, or that
these barriers of disintegration and cataclysms I had felt
rising in me were not the result of an intelligent and or-
ganized premeditation, I had reached one of the last places

in the world where the dance of healing by Peyote still exists, or at least the place where it was invented. And what was it then, what false presentiment, what illusory and artificial intuition caused me to expect some sort of liberation for my body and also and above all a force, an illumination throughout the reaches of my inner landscape, which I felt at that precise minute to be beyond any kind of dimensions?

Twenty-eight days since this inexplicable torment had begun. And twelve days since I had come to this isolated corner of the earth, this tiny compartment in the vast mountain, waiting on the good will of my sorcerers.

Why was it that each time, as at this moment, I felt myself touching on a vitally important phase of my existence, I did not come to it with a whole organism? Why this terrible sensation of loss, of a void to be filled, of an event that miscarries? To be sure, I would see the sorcerers carry out their rite; but in what way would this rite profit me? I would see them. I would be rewarded for this long patience which nothing until then had been able to discourage. Nothing—neither the terrible road, nor the voyage with a body which was intelligent but dissonant and which had to be dragged, which had to be almost killed to prevent it from revolting; nor nature with her sudden storms which surround us with their nets of thunder; nor that long night filled with spasms in which I had seen a young Indian scratch himself in a dream with a kind of hostile frenzy in exactly the places where these spasms seized me—and he said, he who scarcely knew me from the day before, "Ah, let him suffer all the evil that may befall him."

Peyote, as I knew, was not made for Whites. It was necessary at all costs to prevent me from obtaining a cure by this rite which was created to act on the very nature of the spirits. And a White, for these Red men, is one whom the spirits have abandoned. If it was I who benefited from the rite, it meant so much lost for themselves, with their intelligent sheathing of spirit.

So much lost for the spirits. So many spirits that could not be utilized again.

And then there is the matter of the *Tesguino*, that alcohol which requires eight days of fermentation in the jars—and there aren't that many jars or that many arms ready to grind the corn.

Once the alcohol has been drunk, the sorcerers of Peyote become useless and a whole new preparation becomes necessary. But a man of these tribes had died when I arrived at the village, and it was necessary that the rite, the priests, the alcohol, the crosses, the mirrors, the rasping sticks, the jars, and all that extraordinary paraphernalia of the Peyote dance be requisitioned for the benefit of the man who had died.

For now that he was dead his double could not wait for these evil spirits to be neutralized.

And after twenty-eight days of waiting, I now had to endure, throughout one long week, an incredible comedy. All over the mountain there was a hysterical coming and going of messengers who were presumably being sent to the sorcerers. But after the messengers had left, the sorcerers would arrive in person, amazed that nothing was ready. And I discovered that I had been tricked.

They brought me priests who heal with dreams, and who speak after they have dreamed.

"Those of *Ciguri* [the Peyote dance] not good," they said. "They do not *work*. Take these." And they pushed toward me some old men who suddenly broke in two, clicking their amulets strangely under their robes. And I saw that they were not sorcerers but magicians. And I also learned that these false priests were intimate friends of death.

One day this commotion died down without protests, without arguments, without fresh promises on my part. As if all this had been part of the rite and as if the performance had lasted long enough.

I had not come to the heart of the mountain of these Tarahumara Indians to look for memories of painting. I had suffered enough, it seems to me, to be rewarded with a little reality.

However, as the daylight faded, a vision confronted my eyes.

I saw before me "The Nativity" of Hieronymus Bosch, with everything in order and oriented in space, the old porch with its collapsing boards in front of the stable, the fire of the Infant King glowing to the left amid the animals, the scattered farms, and the shepherds; and in the foreground other animals bleating, and to the right the Dancer Kings. The kings, with their crowns of mirrors on their heads and their rectangular purple cloaks on their backs—at my right in the painting—like the Magi of Hieronymus Bosch. And suddenly as I turned around, doubting to the last minute that I would ever see my sorcerers arrive, I saw them coming down the mountain, leaning on huge staffs, their women carrying huge baskets, the servants armed with bundles of crosses like firewood, and mirrors that glittered like segments of sky amid all this apparatus of crosses, pikes, shovels, and tree trunks stripped of their branches. And all these people were bent under the weight of this extraordinary apparatus, and the wives of the sorcerers, like their men, were also leaning on huge staffs a head taller than they were.

Wood fires rose on all sides toward the sky. Below, the dances had already begun; and at the sight of this beauty at last realized, this beauty of glowing imaginations, like voices in an illuminated dungeon, I felt that my effort had not been in vain.

Above, on the slopes of the enormous mountain which descended toward the village in tiers, a circle had been drawn on the ground. The women were already kneeling in front of their *metates* (stone basins), grinding the Peyote with a kind of scrupulous violence. The priests began to trample the circle. They trampled it carefully and in all directions; and in the middle of the circle they kindled a fire that the wind from above sucked up in whorls.

During the day two young goats had been killed. And now I saw, on a branchless tree trunk that had also been carved in the shape of a cross, the lungs and hearts of the animals trembling in the night wind.

Another tree trunk had been placed near the first, and the fire that had been lighted in the middle of the circle drew from it at every moment innumerable flashes of light, something like a fire seen through a pile of thick glasses. When I approached in order to discern the nature of this burning center, I perceived an incredible network of tiny bells, some of silver, others of horn, attached to leather straps which were also awaiting the moment for their ritual use.

On the side where the sun rises they drove into the ground ten crosses of unequal height but arranged in a symmetrical pattern, and to each cross they attached a mirror.

Twenty-eight days of this horrible waiting after the dangerous withdrawal were now culminating in a circle peopled with Beings, here represented by ten crosses.

Ten, of the Number of ten, like the Invisible Masters of Peyote, in the Sierra.

And among these ten: the Male Principle of Nature, which the Indians call *San Ignacio,* and its female, *San Nicolás!*

Around this circle is a zone of moral abandonment in which no Indian would venture: it is told that birds who stray into this circle fall, and that pregnant women feel their embryos rot inside them.

There is a history of the world in the circle of this dance, compressed between two suns, the one that sets and the one that rises. And it is when the sun sets that the sorcerers enter the circle, and that the dancer with the six hundred bells (three hundred of horn and three hundred of silver) utters his coyote's howl in the forest.

The dancer enters and leaves, and yet he does not leave the circle. He moves forward deliberately into evil. He immerses himself in it with a kind of terrible courage, in a rhythm which above the Dance seems to depict the Illness. And one seems to see him alternately emerging and disappearing in a movement which evokes one knows not what obscure tantalizations. He enters and leaves: *"leaves the daylight, in the first chapter,"* as is said of Man's Double in the *Egyptian Book of the Dead.* For this advance into the illness is a voyage, a *descent in order to RE-EMERGE INTO THE DAYLIGHT.* He turns in a circle in the direction of the wings of the Swastika, always from right to left, and from the top.

He leaps with his army of bells, like an agglomeration of dazed bees caked together in a crackling and tempestuous disorder.

Ten crosses in the circle and *ten* mirrors. *One* beam with *three* sorcerers on it. *Four* priests (*two* Males and *two* Females). The epileptic dancer, and *myself,* for whom the rite was being performed.

At the foot of each sorcerer, *one* hole, at the bottom of which the Male and Female principles in Nature, represented by the hermaphroditic roots of the Peyote plant (Peyote, of course, has the shape of the male and female sexual organs combined), lie dormant in Matter, that is, in the Concrete.

And the hole, with a wooden or earthen basin inverted over it, represents rather well the Globe of the World. On the basin, the sorcerers rasp the mixture or the dislocation of the two principles, and they rasp them in the Abstract, that is, in Principle. Whereas beneath, these two Principles, incarnated, repose in Matter, that is, in the Concrete.

And all night long the sorcerers reestablish the lost relationships with triangular gestures that strangely cut off the spatial perspective.

Between the *two* suns, *twelve* tempos in *twelve* phases. And the circular movement of everything that swarms around the fire, within the sacred limits of the circle: the dancer, the rasping sticks, the sorcerers.

After each phase, the sorcerers were eager to perform the physical proof of the rite, to demonstrate the effectiveness of the operation. Hieratic, ritual, sacerdotal, there they stand, lined up on their beam, rocking their rasping sticks like babies. From what idea of a lost formality do they derive the sense of these bows, these nods, this circular movement in which they count their steps, cross themselves in front of the fire, salute one another, and leave?

So they get up, perform the bows I have mentioned, some like men on crutches, others like sawed-off robots. They step outside the circle. But once they have left the circle, before they are a yard outside it, these priests who walk between two suns have suddenly become men again, that is, abject organisms who must be cleansed, whom this rite is designed to cleanse. They behave like well-diggers, these priests, some kind of night laborers created to piss and to relieve themselves. They piss, fart, and relieve themselves with terrible thunderous noises; and to hear them one would think that they had set out to level the real thunder, to reduce it to *their need* for abasement.

Of the three sorcerers who were there, two, the two smallest and shortest, had had the right to handle the rasping stick for three years (for the right to handle the rasp is acquired, and in fact this right determines the nobility of the caste of the Peyote sorcerers among the Tarahumara Indians); and the third had had the right for ten years. And I must admit that it was the one most experienced in the rite who pissed the best and who farted the loudest and most expressively.

And a few moments later the same man, with the pride of this manner of crude purgation, began to spit. He spat after drinking the Peyote, as we all did. For after the twelve phases of the dance had been performed, and since dawn was about to break, we were passed the ground-up Peyote, which was like a kind of muddy gruel; and in front of each of us a new hole was dug to receive the spit from our mouths, which contact with the Peyote had henceforth made sacred.

"Spit," the dancer told me, "but as deep in the ground as possible, for no particle of *Ciguri* must ever emerge again."

And it was the sorcerer who had grown old in the harness who spat most abundantly and with the largest and most compact gobs. And the other sorcerers and the dancer, gathered in a circle around the hole, had come to admire him.

After I had spat, I fell to the ground, overcome with drowsiness. The dancer in front of me passed back and forth endlessly, turning and crying *unnecessarily*, because he had discovered that his cry pleased me.

"Get up, man, get up," he shouted each time he passed me, with diminishing effect.

Aroused and staggering, I was led toward the crosses for the final cure, in which the sorcerers shake the rasp on the very head of the patient.

Thus I took part in the rite of water, the rite of the blows on the skull, the rite of that kind of mutual cure which the participants give each other, the rite of immoderate ablutions.

They uttered strange words over my head while sprinkling me with water; then they sprinkled each other nervously, for the mixture of corn liquor and Peyote was beginning to make them wild.

And it was with these final movements that the Peyote dance ended.

The Peyote dance is contained in the rasping stick, in this wood steeped in time which has absorbed the secret salts of the earth. In this wand that is held out and withdrawn lies the curative power of this rite, which is so remote and which must be hunted down like a beast in the forest.

There is an out-of-the-way spot in the high Mexican Sierra where these rasping sticks seemingly abound. They sleep there, waiting for the Predestined Man to discover them and bring them *into the light of day*.

When a Tarahumara sorcerer dies, he takes leave of his rasping stick with infinitely more sorrow than he feels in leaving his body; and his descendants and intimates take the rasp away and bury it in this sacred corner of the forest.

When a Tarahumara Indian believes that he is called upon to handle the rasp and distribute the cure, he goes to spend a week in the forest at Easter time every year for three years.

It is there, they say, that the Invisible Master of Peyote speaks to him with his nine advisers, and that he passes the secret on to him. And he emerges with the rasping stick properly macerated.

Carved out of the wood of a tree that grew in warm soil,

gray as iron ore, it carries notches on its length and signs at its two extremities, four triangles with one point for the Male Principle and two points for the Female of Nature, made divine.

One notch for every year the sorcerer was alive after he had acquired the right to handle the rasp and had become a master capable of performing those acts of exorcism which pull the Elements apart.

And this is precisely the aspect of this mysterious tradition which I did not succeed in penetrating. For the Peyote sorcerers seem truly to have gained something at the end of their three years of retreats in the forest.

There is a mystery here which the Tarahumara sorcerers have until now jealously guarded. Of what they have acquired in addition, what they have *recovered*, if you will, no Tarahumara Indian who is not a member of the aristocracy of the sect seems to have the slightest idea. And as for the sorcerers themselves, on this point they are resolutely silent.

What is the singular word, the lost word which the Master of Peyote communicates to them? And why does it take the Tarahumara sorcerers three years to be able to handle the rasp, with which, it must be admitted, they perform some very curious *auscultations*?

What is it, then, which they have wrested from the forest, and which the forest *yields to them so slowly*?

In short, what has been communicated to them which is not contained in the external apparatus of the rite, and which neither the piercing cries of the dancer, nor his dance, which goes back and forth like a kind of epileptic pendulum, nor the circle, nor the fire in the middle of the

circle, nor the crosses with their mirrors in which the dis-
torted heads of the sorcerers alternately swell and disappear into the flames of the fire, nor the night wind that
speaks and blows on the mirrors, nor the chant of the sorcerers rocking their rasps, that astonishingly vulnerable
and intimate chant, can succeed in explaining?

They had laid me on the ground at the foot of that enormous beam on which the three sorcerers were sitting during the dances.

On the ground, so that the rite would fall on me, so that
the fire, the chants, the cries, the dance, and the night
itself, would turn over me like a living, human vault.
There was this rolling vault, this physical arrangement of
cries, tones, steps, chants. But above everything, beyond
everything, the recurring impression that behind all this,
greater than all this and beyond it, there was concealed
something else: *the Principal.*

I did not renounce as a group those dangerous dissoci-
ations which Peyote seems to provoke and which I had
pursued for twenty years by other means; I did not mount
my horse with a body pulled out of itself and which the
withdrawal to which I had abandoned myself deprived
henceforth of its essential reflexes; I was not that man of
stone whom it required two men to turn into a man on
horseback: and who was mounted on and dismounted from
the horse like a broken robot—and once I was on the horse,
they placed my hands on the reins, and they also had to
close my fingers around the reins, for left to myself it was
only too clear that I had lost the use of them; I had not
conquered by strength of mind that invincible organic
hostility in which it was *I* who no longer wanted to func-

tion, only to bring back a collection of outworn imageries from which the Age, true to its own system, would at most derive ideas for advertisements and models for clothing designers. It was now necessary that what lay hidden behind this heavy grinding which reduces dawn to darkness —that this thing be pulled out, and that it *serve,* that it serve precisely by *my crucifixion.*

To this I knew that my physical destiny was irrevocably bound. I was ready for any burning, and I awaited the first fruits of the fire in view of a conflagration that would soon be universal.

The Land of the Magi Kings

✳

WHERE HAD I HEARD that it was not in Italy but in Mexico that the pre-Renaissance painters found the blue of their landscapes, and the vast perspectives of the backgrounds with which they embellished their Nativities?

In the land of the Tarahumara the most incredible legends offer proofs of their own reality. When one enters this landscape and finds gods at the tops of mountains, gods with an arm hacked off on the left side and an empty space on the right side, and who lean to the right; and when, bending down, one hears rising at one's feet the roar of a waterfall, and above the fall a wind that rushes from peak to peak, and when one climbs until one can see around one a vast circle of peaks, one can no longer doubt that one has arrived at one of those sensitive points on the earth where life has shown her first effects.

The pre-Renaissance painters of Italy were initiated into a secret science which modern science has not yet completely rediscovered, and this science was also known to the artists of the High Renaissance.

The blue of the remote backdrops of the high mountains of Mexico evokes precise forms and ideas, it compels the mind to revive the distant memory of a Science to which the

APPEARANCE OF THE THREE MAGI KINGS IS CONNECTED!!!!

It was not out of a religious spirit that the Piero della Francescas, the Lucas van Leydens, the Fra Angelicos, the Piero di Cosimos, or the Mantegnas painted so many Nativities. It was because of a traditional preoccupation with the Essential, a diligent pursuit of the secrets of life, and because of that natural obsession of Great Minds with the How and the Why of those first principles and first explosions of Nature which were expressed in the *Pagan legend of Christmas*.

If Religion later took over these principles and if the masses were weak enough to turn away from the Principles and to worship religion instead, so much the worse for the foolish and fanatical masses; but this in no way weakens the Principles. In the Tarahumara mountain everything speaks only of the Essential, that is, of the principles according to which Nature was created; and everything lives only for these principles: the People, the storms, the wind, the silence, the sun.

We are far from the warlike and civilized reality of the modern world, and not warlike although civilized, but warlike *because civilized:* this is how the Tarahumara think. And their legends, or rather *their Traditions* (for here there are no legends, no imaginary fables, but Traditions which may be incredible, but whose reality is gradually being proved by the excavations of scholars), their traditions tell of the appearance among the Tarahumara tribes of a race of fire-bearing Men who had three Masters or Kings who traveled toward the Pole Star.

But if Science has its Masters—Newton, Darwin, Kepler, Lavoisier, etc.—Civilizations also have their Masters,

from the moral and Social point of view—Odin, Rama,
Fu Hsi, Lao-tzu, Zoroaster, Confucius—and the legend of
the Three Magi Kings seems to conceal the journey through
the geographic line of the great Solar Tradition, wherever
Scientific Worship of the Sun has left its mathematically
oriented pyramids and altars, of three Civilizers who were
initiated into a transcendent astronomy whose laws were
comparable to those of Mayan astronomy.

When one knows that astronomical worship of the sun
has been universally expressed by signs, and that these
signs are identical to those of an ancient and very complete science which the absurd language of Europe has
designated as UNIVERSAL ESOTERISM; and that these
signs—the anserated cross, the Swastika, the Double cross,
the large circle with a dot in the middle, the two opposing
triangles, the three dots, the four triangles at the four
cardinal points, the twelve signs of the zodiac, etc.—are
found in profusion in the East as well as in Mexico, on
temples and in manuscripts (but never have I seen them
abound *in Nature* as they do in the heart of the Tarahumara mountain); when one knows this and when one
suddenly finds oneself in a country that is literally haunted
by these signs, and when one recognizes them in the gestures and rites of a race, and when the men, women, and
children of this race wear them embroidered on their clothing, one feels uneasy, as if one had arrived at the source
of a mystery.

But when one also considers that the Tarahumara Sierra
is the land where the first skeletons of gigantic men were
found, and that at the very moment I am writing, more
are constantly being found, many legends lose their leg-

endary appearance and become realities. A reality which
may have had its superhuman laws, although they were
based on nature, was rejected by the Renaissance of the
sixteenth century; and the Humanism of the Renaissance
was not an expansion but a diminution of man, since Man
stopped raising himself to the level of nature and brought
nature down to his own size, and an exclusive concern
with the human brought about the loss of the Natural.

It was then that the astronomical science of nature, according to which life revolves around the Sun, became occult; but in this magical naturalism which is everywhere
the same and whose tradition is working its way steadily
from the east to the west, the Primitives of Florence, Assisi,
Como, etc., were initiated.

In their canvases of Nativities and of the Magi Kings,
these painters expressed a mystery of life, and they expressed it as the heirs of an age in which Art was primarily
the servant of a science; this is why their paintings, although they may be read with the affective fibers of the
soul, may also be read with the high rational Science of
the mind. A color, if it enchants the heart, corresponds to
an exact and scientific vibration in which the Primal Numbers can be found.

And so it struck me as more than strange that the land
in which the tradition of the Magi as fire-bearers lives on
the face of the rocks, and in the clothing and the sacred
rites of the people, is also the land in which the colorful
rhythm and the awesome vibration of Nature recall with
the most haunting intensity a whole age of painting whose
Masters were obsessed with the same signs, the same
forms, the same lights, the same secrets.

Nature has produced the dancers in their circle just as she produces corn in its circle and the signs in the forests.*

* Sentence jotted down by Artaud on the verso of the seventh leaf of the manuscript of *The Land of the Magi Kings*.

The Rite of the Kings
of Atlantis

*

On THE 16TH OF SEPTEMBER, the day on which Mexicans celebrate their independence, I saw in Norogachic, in the heart of the Tarahumara Sierra, the rite of the kings of Atlantis as Plato describes it in the pages of *Critias*. Plato talks about a strange rite which, because of circumstances that threatened the future of their race, was performed by the kings of Atlantis.

However mythical the existence of Atlantis may be, Plato describes the Atlanteans as a race of magical origin. The Tarahumara, whom I believe to be the direct descendants of the Atlanteans, continue to devote themselves to the observance of magical rites.

Let those who do not believe me go into the Tarahumara Sierra: they will see that, in this land where the rocks have the appearance and structure of a fable, legend becomes reality and that there can be no reality outside of this fable. I know that the life of the Indians is not to the taste of the modern world; however, in the presence of a race like this one, we must conclude that it is modern life which is backward in relation to something else, and not

the Tarahumara Indians who are backward in relation
to the modern world.

They know that every step forward, every convenience
acquired through the mastery of a purely physical civilization, also implies a loss, a regression.

As a consequence, one can say that in the presence of
any authentic tradition the question of progress does not
arise. Real traditions do not progress, since they represent
the most advanced stage of every truth. The only progress
that can be made consists in preserving the form and the
force of these traditions. Down through the centuries, the
Tarahumara have been able to learn how to preserve their
virility.

To return to Plato and the true esoteric traditions found
in his written works, I saw in the Tarahumara mountain
the rite of these visionary and desperate kings.

Plato relates that at sunset the kings of Atlantis gathered
in front of a bull that had been sacrificed. And while attendants carved the bull into pieces, other attendants collected the pieces and poured the blood into cups. The kings
drank this blood and became intoxicated as they sang a
kind of plaintive melody until there was nothing left in
the sky but the head of the dying sun and nothing left on
earth but the head of the sacrificed bull. Then the kings
covered their heads with ashes. And their plaintive melody
changed in tone as they tightened the circle they had
formed. Every invocation to the sun became a kind of
bitter reproach, took on the appearance of a public penance, a kind of remorse which the kings expressed with a
common accord until darkness had completely fallen.

This is the essence of the rite described by Plato. Well,

shortly before the sun went down over Norogachic, the Indians led an ox to the village square and, after tying its feet, began to cut out its heart. The fresh blood was caught in large jars. I shall not easily forget the ox's grimace of pain as the Indian's knife ripped open its bowels. The matachín dancers gathered in front of the bull and when he was dead they began their flower dances.

For the Indians perform dances of flowers, dragonflies, birds, and many other things in front of this butchery, and it was truly a strange spectacle to see two Indians mounted on the dead bull, collecting the blood and cutting off chunks of flesh with axes, while other Indians dressed like kings with crowns of mirrors on their heads performed their dances of dragonflies, birds, wind, objects, flowers.

The dancing went on until the middle of the night.

A whole village may participate in the matachín dances, but there is a king for each moment of the dance. And the dancer kings take turns: each dances according to his temperament.

That day there was only one musician, who sat on the ground and played the violin. But the full orchestra consisted of a guitar, a small drum, bells, and iron bars. The small drum is a musical instrument of war; its sound reverberates from peak to peak.

The kings of the dance wear crowns of mirrors, the triangular Masonic apron, and a large rectangular mantle over their shoulders. They also have special trousers with a triangular design at the bottom, which comes a little below the knee.

The matachins are not a sacred rite but a popular and profane dance which was brought to Mexico by the Span-

ish; but the Tarahumara have given it an Indian form,
they have stamped it with their own spirit. Although originally these dances imitate the movements of external nature—wind, trees, an anthill, a rushing river—among the
Tarahumara they take on a highly cosmogonic meaning,
and I felt as if I had before me and were contemplating
a mass of planetary ants swarming to the rhythm of a
celestial music.

They dance to the sound of a childlike and subtle music
that no European ear can perceive; at first, it seems as if
one is always hearing the same sound, set to the same
rhythm; but with time, these identical sounds and this
rhythm awaken in us something resembling the memory
of a great myth; they evoke the sense of a mysterious and
complicated history.

The leader of the dance contorted his body in time to
the rhythm, and his dance imitated the step of a tiny ant
tottering; the dancer bent double, contracted with the spas-
tic movements of an enormously swollen frog; his right
hand skillfully balanced a gourd full of rings made of hard-
ened caterpillars which had taken on the consistency of
glass, while his left hand played with a fan of flowers.

The music of the Tarahumara is divided into a very
limited number of tempos which are repeated indefinitely.
Each time the beat changes, the leader of the dance leaves
his place, abandons the spot where he was making his
contorted movements, and begins to circle around the
other dancers.

These dancers are divided into two groups, and each
dancer in turn presents his face to the leader. He does this
like a knight in armor, with the splendor of the ancient

warrior in full battle dress, then he turns and faces the opposite direction. When the leader of the dance has circled around each dancer, he prances back to his place. And one phase of the dance is over. But others take its place and the frenzy resumes and continues all night, from the instant the sun goes down until dawn, without the dancers ever becoming tired.

A row of young people leaning sideways against the wall —that is, not with their backs against the wall, but showing sometimes the left side, sometimes the right—now and then utter a frozen cry like a hunting horn in the forest, and their voices evoke the mournful sound of a hyena, a sick dog, or a strangled cock. This cry is not emitted continuously but at intervals; it passes from mouth to mouth like a human scale which takes on in the darkness the quality of a summons.

They danced this way until sunset, and while they danced, other Indians picked up the pieces of the bull's body, leaving the head alone on the ground at the very moment when the sun's head sank in the sky. It was then that the leaders of the dance stopped, and the dancers formed a circle around them. And they all took up again a kind of plaintive melody. A melody of remorse, of religious penance, a secret summons to I know not what dark forces, what presences from *the beyond*.

Next they went and sat down in front of a large fire at some distance from the first place, in a spot that was covered and closed in like the night itself, for the second part of the rite was to demonstrate its secrecy. It was at this moment that they were given the living blood, served in cups. And the dance began again from the beginning and went on all night.

The chunks of beef had been collected in four jars, and over the jars the women formed a huge cross. Everyone drank the warm blood and endlessly repeated the froglike movements. At times everyone would be asleep. Then the violin would offer its music and the dancing would begin again. And the men, joining in now and then, would scream like strangled jackals.

You may think what you will of the comparison I am making. In any case, since Plato never went to Mexico and since the Tarahumara Indians never saw him, it must be acknowledged that the idea of this sacred rite came to them from the same fabulous and prehistoric source. And this is what I have tried to suggest here.

[Artaud's published Spanish text was translated into French by Marie Dézon and Philippe Sollers, from which this translation was made. —Tr.]

*

Supplement to a Voyage to the Land of the Tarahumara

*

HUMAN CONSCIOUSNESS has the right to ask itself many questions, and I have asked myself many all over the world, including even that ultimate interrogation in which consciousness and question disappear and there is only the indescribable flame that shoots out of the mind of God each time His Heart is alerted.

For anyone who pursues the mental side of things with his heart, there is a point, as in the Peyote rite of the Tarahumara, when the fabric of perception opens in a cross, and cracks in such a way that one no longer knows whether it is from one's own heart that this cross has emerged, or from the heart of that Other, who then is no longer the Other, *any* Other, but THAT ONE, the Only Source of Flames, whose tongue pierces and gathers the taste for the Word, when the heart which was beating like a Double, recognizes its GENERATOR!

For if there is neither God nor problem, then neither is there a heart to perceive nor a heart to tear the perception that pierces, and to tear *itself* into a cross in the midst of perception.

Because I kept seeing around me men lying, lying about the source of idea, idiotically refusing to advance as far as ideas, I felt the need to leave mankind and to go away to a place where I could at last freely advance with my heart, all of this heart which before my attentive mind gathers and sweeps away the emotions of images which come to it from the circular Absolute, that woven tide which pierces my spinal column and which my heart then flings back toward my solar plexus with a spasm like the sea.

What constitutes the Self, I have no idea. Consciousness? A horrible repulsion before the Nameless, the unwoven, for the I comes when the heart has knotted it at last, chosen, *drawn* out of this and that, against this and *for* that, despite the eternal calculation of horrors with which all the non-selves, demons, assail that which will be my being, this being which I continue to see failing before my eyes as long as God has not passed his key to my heart.

One sees God when one really wants to, and to see God is to be dissatisfied with the little enclave of terrestrial sensations which have never done anything but slightly expand the hunger for a self and for a whole consciousness which the world does not cease to murder and betray.

One day I was far from God, but at the same time never had I felt so far from my own consciousness, and I saw that without God there is neither consciousness nor being, and that the man who believes himself to be still living can never again reenter himself.

So it was that, growing toward God, I discovered the Tarahumara.

The highest idea of human consciousness and of its universal answers—Absolute, Eternity, Infinite—still exists in this race of old Indians who say they have received the Sun in order to transmit it to the deserving, and who in the Rites of Ciguri have preserved the organic gate of that ordeal by which our being, which the impure assembly of beings has rejected, knows that it is connected with that place beyond bodily perceptions where the Heart of the Divine burns to summon us.

I do not know how many suns all the initiatory doctrines of the earth, whose sole source I know and it is called JESUS CHRIST, claim to have recognized, from the first to the sixth sun, but it is clear that the Tarahumara of Mexico have not yet fallen from the first, for they have preserved within themselves the flaming image of that Source which they call the Son of God. One day, say the priests of TUTU-GURI, the Great Celestial Healer appeared as if born out of the open lips of the Sun, THE DESIRING, His Father in Eternity. And He was Himself this sun, bearing in his hand The First Cross, and He struck a blow; and other Solar Crosses, and Doubles of Suns, were born out of Him, and came out at each Syllable which this Mouth of Celestial Crosses imprinted on the immensity in hosts of light.

Six times the Cross of light struck and the sun rebounded in space. And the last sun was incorruptible and pure, as one sees it still over the sea and the land, but even at the first sun the darkness had reentered the light, for the Son of the Desiring, having reascended to his Father, had resumed with Him his journey through Eternity.

Now this is the true Story of Jesus Christ as it has been handed down to us in the teachings of the original Christianity of the Catacombs, and I wanted to see whether,

behind the sacred memory of those Rites which I know not
what paganism has overlaid, the Tarahumara of the modern age would recognize their Initiator.

And an impression of the true face of Christ was shown
them, the same one that was imprinted on the veil of St.
Veronica in the march toward Golgotha; and after mysteriously conferring, the priests of TUTUGURI came and told
me that this was indeed his face, and that it was in this
form that the Son of God had once appeared to the an-
cestors of their fathers.

And this Healer of the Infinite had given them a plant
on his Travels, in order to reopen for the tempted and tired
soul the gates of Eternity. And this plant is CIGURI.

For the soul goes from day to night, like the earth; only
the sun goes from light to light; for him there is only the
day, and night is that which is always far from him. But
who shall say at night that there is no sun? Who shall say,
when the heavens are dense with clouds, that no sun has
ever overcome them? Today this is all that people say
about someone whom I have seen as truly as I see the sun;
and I do not doubt it on rainy days! This Someone, all
those whom I love on this earth have desired him with
me, and missed him; and they and I have revolved an im-
measurable time as if in the lost trail of a star, until this
star has exploded before the human eye, and until we have
finally seen it explode. And whoever among my friends
and my brothers has seen this sun explode, someday he
too will remember it and say it, and what a beautiful day
that will be. As for the others, they will have become too
much like animals in order to obscure the Truth.

—It often happens that night rises darkly over the soul and in such a way that the soul, driven by temptation and weary, no longer remembers clearly whence it came: from above or from below, from the light or from the shadows. It is at such times that the Peyote given by Jesus Christ intervenes. It snatches the soul from behind and sets it again in the eternal light, as it proceeds from the Spirit on high; and maintaining it in this On-High it teaches the soul to distinguish between itself and that unfathomable energy which is as the infinite multiple of its own capacities and which begins where we, those millions upon millions called beings, burn out and run dry.

—No matter how high I have risen in the shadows of the mind, I am not always conscious of having decided for the clearest reasons in favor of this or that. There is between the self and the non-self a conflict which the ages have not yet resolved. The Illusory, which I do not like, often gives me the impression that it occupies my consciousness with a seductive vigor much stronger than the Real. This is because before me there is temptation: the temptation to be this or that, like this or like that, this one or that one. This is the reason for that terrible battle which in the foreconscious of my Will and of my Acts I have always waged with that which was not me. But who is to tell me by virtue of what I have decided to choose my consciousness. Man experiences Good and Evil as if a force dictated them to him, but he has never seen himself at the Source that distributes those nameless impulses that cause him to judge and to prefer. When he does Good he judges it to be better, reassuring, and very preferable, but when he does Evil, or when for an instant he considers it, he wonders if it is not by chance Evil which might be the better, and for what reasons, the very reasons that disappeared from his mind which Evil has just plunged in darkness, the Good was conceived by him as Good and Evil as bad, whereas God, only a little further away than he claims to believe that he lives, has never ceased to tell him so. But God is that which he has never wanted to hear.

—In accepting himself in this way without curiosity about God and without problems, man is now nothing but an inert automaton, generating boredom and madness, which all consciousness has abandoned, and which the still pure soul has fled, because it senses in advance the moment when this Automaton will give birth to the Beast, and the Beast to an obscene demon.

I felt, therefore, that I should go back to the source and expand my pre-consciousness to the point where I would see myself evolve and *desire*. And Peyote led me to this point. Transported by Peyote I saw that I had to defend what I am before I was born, and that my Self is merely the consequence of the battle I waged in the Supreme against the untruth of evil ideas.

And human beings can drone on and on that things are as they are and that there is nothing else to look for; for myself, I see clearly that they have lost their footing, and that *they don't know what they are saying*, and have not for a long time, for they have forgotten the source of those mental states with which they hold themselves above the flow of ideas, and which are the basis of language.

Indeed, it has been centuries since their thinkers, like the rest, abdicated the honorable effort that is involved in earning one's consciousness, once one knows *where* it must be won.

—The Unconscious does not belong to me except in dreams, and then, everything that I see in it and that lingers—is it a form selected to be born, or something unclean that I have rejected?

The Subconscious is that which is exhaled by the first premises of my inner Will, but I am not sure who reigns there, and I believe that it is not me, but that mass of opposing Wills which, I don't know why, thinks inside me, and has never had any other preoccupation or any other idea in the world than to take my own place in my body and in my self.

But in the Pre-conscious in which their Temptations abuse me, I see all these evil wills again, but armed this time with all my consciousness, and what does it matter if they unfurl it against me, since now I feel that I am there?

In the Pre-conscious, Peyote will hold me, and above the state of man I shall know from what source my Will was formed, and by what force it fell back in the direction in which the Good calls, against the Evil which was pursuing it.

Good and Evil, say the priests of Ciguri—as later the Mystics of Jesus Christ restated it, no longer in terms of sensations and visions, but with the evidence of martyrdom and the experience of their wounds—Good and Evil are not two opposing fabrics or principles; Good is that which exists and Evil that which does not exist, which will not live, and which will cease. The Self of man will not believe in it always. But this science he has yet to attain.

And it would appear that the purpose of the Peyote Dance, originally a Rite designed to reveal the teachings of the Plant given to man by Jesus Christ, was to invite the human creature to arrive at consciousness. For without help he cannot make up his mind to it.

It has taken thousands of years of trials for the soul to recognize what it accepted or rejected in this unleashing of powerful appetites in which consciousness is constantly atoning and being born above any figure of Purity or of Sin.

I live and I was born with the limitless temptation of being: what shall I be, where did I come from, where am I going and how? And I do not know whether at my death I shall have stopped choosing, struggling, rejecting. But why must all my impulses toward the beyond, toward openness, always be mingled with these calculations of the unspeakable, these insinuations of a base eroticism?

Shall I, then, never again see things in the light of chastity in which they were born? Why is my pure temptation to be and to live joined with this foul aspiration to exist only by and in Sin?

Man today is unclean and impure. He cannot distinguish between the base and the Sublime, between eroticism and Poetry.

One day I decided to throw off this abominable enslavement which I knew very well did not come from me, but had been imposed on me by that infernal coalition of creatures who have taken over and polluted our consciousness just as they are disordering Reality.

And I saw, on the mountains of Mexico, above all human trials, the glowing flames of a Great Bleeding Heart.

Caught, as I rose, as if by the arm of the sea, I saw myself flung back outside of the uncertain conformity of things, and *laid out* as I am at last, myself, in the Truth of the Essential.

Behind Ciguri there is completion, plethora, the plethora of fulfillment.

But at the bottom of Ciguri, and in this Flaming Heart a Form in which I could not help recognizing JESUS CHRIST: the perception of the complete Unalterable, the entire Cross, incorruptibly spreads, at the Cardinal Points of all Satiety.

With JESUS CHRIST-PEYOTE, I *heard* the human body, Spleen, Liver, Lungs, Brain, thundering at the four corners of the Divine Infinite. And what extraordinary necessity dictated their organic arrangement.

But internally replaced in the stature of my limbs, I saw the Cross of Calvary appear like a bloody rending of organs, which has enabled the human mind to grasp, by the virtues of this very blood, its own, the shoals of Eternity.

And this cross explained to me human consciousness. And with the help of Ciguri of the cross I saw the original prototypes of every state and every form swell to that point of terrible explosion where the soul of man is cut into four parts at the very moment it realizes that it is going to fall into this opacity which has the face of Sin. For to hold oneself in consciousness is to hold oneself above Sin. And nothing has the right to be called consciousness except that which has been able never to leave the shoal of Eternity. Outside of this the human being will founder, however strongly he believes that he is still alive, when the Seers see him already delivered.

With Ciguri-Jesus Christ I saw, steeped in high thunderclouds, all that is consciousness and being, and below, in the non-existent, that image in which the debased consciousness of man believed it molded sexuality. For it is sexuality which is sin. And to touch it is to run away from being and sink into the void.

It was thus that my experience with Peyote saved me from the void and that, once I had gone beyond the cross of the spasm in which my heart by bursting was made new, I went behind things at the place where the Virgin of the Eternal struck me, then sent me back, and I reemerged on earth as if struck by lightning in my mind.

I had in no sense touched God, of course, for it is not by means of a physiological experiment that one arrives at Divinity; but I had understood one of the essential Laws by which his Force in transmitting itself has ordered the tenor of Existence, and that is the law of Purity.

Be chaste or perish, this is what I learned while I was with the Tarahumara of the mountain, but which Evil had caused even them to forget.

And this Law is not peculiar to me, but it was made for all men from the beginning of time and for all time. And I know that we shall see it again and that now it will not go away. And that man before he leaves the earth will sweat his blood because of this Law.

As for God, All the Rigorous Eminence which nothing in the world can take away, it is not in the Unreal but in the Real that one finds him, however far beyond ordinary consciousness his Reality may be. But the Supreme Divine Reality is at the bottom of the heart of every man for whom Love is *loving*. Loving from the heart; giving without taking. Something which the senses cannot do. And which the world of earthly life has refused to realize.

Those who say that there is no God do so because they have forgotten the heart.

The infinite emulsion of the heart is what Evil has tried to kill in the worlds, but in this emulsion there are many folds, thicknesses, substances, and textures, and each thickness is an idea, and the idea a state of the heart, and a creature with its own soul, and each state of the sensible a substance that has come out of God, and the Source of all Substance this Giving Heart, Distributor of substances of being who gives its substance to Being in the Multiformity of the Infinite. And where would he die, He who could not be killed? For besides being the Idea of the Eternally Renascent, God is also Someone; and this someone is the inexhaustible Active who, over all sleep and all dreams, swallows that which, in the further of Him-Self, later, He will give! Later. In that later in which there burst forth the Word, his Son, in Flames of Love that will never fail.

And it was this God of Eternal Charity whom the following year I went to find among the Irish.

Appendix

THE PRIESTS of Ciguri have a strange doctrine which strangely resembles that doctrine of Grace which two hundred years ago provoked the bitterest struggles. But it provoked much worse struggles, this time not in intellectual debates or in words but in events, in the period following the death of Jesus Christ. But these struggles have been forgotten. And yet . . .

The priests of Ciguri say that Peyote is not given to everyone and that to have access to it one must be *Predestined*. For Ciguri is a God jealous of his science and he does not allow this science to be forgotten. But the states through which Peyote forces one to go constitute a disorientation of terrible rigor. Anyone who, after emerging from these states, has lost some part of them, can no longer be entitled to the Word, because without meaning to he will lie about the Essential. And the Essential is the gatekeeper of God.

But Ciguri defends itself, and anyone who has not entered into it with a relatively pure conscience will surrender all the essential parts of his conscience to the Infinite, since he is unworthy to keep them. As for the unworthy, he will remain at the door. And to enter into Peyote with a bad conscience is to expose oneself to a terrible correction.

＊

A Note on Peyote

＊

I took Peyote in the mountains of Mexico, and I had a dose of it that lasted me two or three days with the Tarahumara, and at the time those three days seemed like the happiest days of my life.

I had stopped tormenting myself, trying to find a reason for my life, and I had stopped having to carry my body around.

I realized that I was inventing life, that that was my function and my *raison d'être*, and that I suffered when my imagination failed, and Peyote gave it to me.

A human being stepped forward and drew the Peyote out of me with a blow.

I made it into real shreds, and the cadaver of a man was torn to shreds and found torn to shreds, somewhere.

rai da kanka da kum
a kum da na kum vönoh

Granting that this world is not the reverse of the other and still less its half,

this world is also a real machinery of which I have

the controls, it is a true factory whose key is inborn humor.

sana tafan tana
tanaf tamafts bai

*

Letters concerning the Tarahumara

*

To Jean Paulhan

Paris, February 4, 1937

Dear friend,

Having arrived at the heart of the Tarahumara mountain, I was struck by physical reminiscences so compelling that they seemed to evoke direct personal memories. Everything—the life of the ground and of the grass below, the jagged profile of the mountain, the particular shapes of the rocks, and above all, the haziness of those layers of light in the unending perspective of peaks ranged one above the other, farther and farther back, in an unimaginable distance—everything seemed to represent an experience I had had before, an experience that had already passed through me, rather than the discovery of a world that was strange but new. All this was not new. The sense of *déjà vu* is vague, I mean *undated;* my impression was precisely situated; for this organic experience that I had had before recalled another to which I felt connected, perhaps indirectly, but all the same by tangible bonds. These were reminiscences of history that came to me from each rock, each plant, each horizon. I did not invent the apparition of the Magi Kings: it was *painstakingly* imposed on me by a landscape constructed like the landscapes in painting, which certainly do not come from nothing. I do not believe in an absolute imagination, I mean one that makes something out of nothing, for me there is no mental image that is not the detached member of an image that has been lived and experienced somewhere. And so these vast, uninhabited images evoked in me others which were once populated, and their life seemed to me to unfold on an extraordinary level; it was not I who invented the tradition of magical signs, and that this mountain was haunted by them is a fact; I made a preliminary attempt at their nomenclature in one of the articles I sent you, but stone by stone, in the final analysis, and at the end of the trip, I had the impression that I had recorded them all: starting with the ╱ which is cut into ╱╱, broken in the middle by a bar ╟ with opposite it the same straight line that came out of it ⟨╫⟩ ; and I can't help it if this H shape which seems to result is the central form around which Plato tells us that the Atlanteans had built their towns. You may find it childish, but it exists in the Tarahumara mountain and in Plato; I saw a rock striped with three vertical bars, 3, and on top of it a smaller one striped with a single bar; I saw the enormous phallic tooth I already told you about with 3 stones on the top and 4 holes on the side; I saw, in a cleft in a rock, the circular head of a man where at dawn the solar disk fits exactly, and below, the man's body lengthened *in shadows* with the right arm extended like a bar of light, and the left like the same bar, but made of shadows too, and bent; I saw the figure of death as if *uprooted* from the surrounding rocks, and in its enormous left hand it held an infant; and I am not mentioning all

the images and all the resemblances I saw, which revealed
a forgotten fauna of nature; which seemed to recall cen-
turies-old myths in which man, having been *tamed*, con-
verses with the Kingdoms that have subdued him; and if
the universal world of the Jews is represented by two over-
lapping triangles, the world of all the Races of red origin
is symbolized by two triangles connected by the ideal line
of a tree; this world I saw a hundred times on the rocks,
born of I know not what astonishing accident of nature;
on the trees: imprinted by the hand of man himself; and
wherever I encountered this famous */*, which is, in fact,
the H of generation, I saw emerging and as if *drawn out*
of trees that had been burned from top to bottom to bring
out their shape, I saw the shape of a man and woman
facing each other, and the man's penis was erect; how
many times did I encounter the little world of the earth
represented by a circle and around this circle the much
vaster one of the indeterminate Universe; how many times
did I come upon the cross of the Rosicrucian tradition: 4
triangles pointing toward the 4 cardinal points and all
centered around a point; I saw this sign! Can I help it if
it corresponds to the cross of the Rosicrucian tradition, if
this is the way it is revealed to us that the Rosicrucians
formed their crosses? And this symbol was repeated a
thousand times, not only in uninhabited Nature, but on
the doors of houses made of a single piece of wood; but on
walls, in the shadows of roofs; I saw houses whose façades
were related to one another by means of squares and dots,
and sometimes by means of rectangles stacked one on top
of the other in piles which seemed to grow taller; and was
I not told in the mountain that these scattered geometrical

figures were not scattered but *united,* and that they constituted the Signs of a language based on the very shape of
breath when it is released in sound? The universal magic
is not founded on many more elementary signs than
those which I encountered in the raw and in nature in a
mountain which even aside from these signs has the light
of a haunted land. It required much less for novelists and
poets to discover and describe myths which their imagination alone invented; in recounting my voyage I have not
pretended to write a scholarly thesis, to trace the path of
a solid tradition, or to furnish proofs to corroborate it; if
people draw their own conclusions from these encounters,
it doesn't matter; and it doesn't really matter to me whether
the Magi Kings on their way home made a side trip through
the uninhabited mountains of Mexico; but I know that
once I got up there, overlooking almost infinite miles of
landscape, I felt stirring strongly within me strange reminiscences and images which at the time I started out I
could never have foreseen. And seeing in these mountains
encrusted with more shapes than the walls of certain
temples in India have divinities, seeing men go by in headbands, men wrapped in mantles which also had embroidered on them triangles, crosses, dots, circles, teardrops,
and streaks of lightning; and these crosses, these dots,
these circles, these rectangles, these teardrops and these
zigzag stripes were by no means distributed at random
like decorative shapes in a symmetry which would have
robbed them of all their meaning, but never did I see 2
mantles bearing the same signs, and each was the color of
the *uneducated face* of the man who wore it; seeing these
men go by apparently ignorant of the symbolism in which

their lives seemed steeped, I could not believe that all this represented any kind of effort or study on their part, or was the result of a conscious and open-eyed premeditation; they did these things, they said, because their fathers did them, and from father to father I wondered to what source these practices could be traced; the most unquestioning brain would have asked itself where these vestiges could have come from and what more than human tradition their presence signified.

Green and yellow are, are they not, the opposing colors of death: green for resurrection, yellow for decomposition, decay, and if coincidences mean anything you will in conclusion allow me to draw your attention to the phenomenon which I am going to relate.

I arrived at nightfall in one of those villages dominated by phalluses, those phalluses stamped with figures which seem to have been put there by a natural accident; someone, I don't know who, was whistling the melody of a Tarahumara dance, 5 high-pitched measures which suddenly fall down a hundred stories, and then a voice replies as if out of the depths; a child walked toward us, all alone, naked under a gray mantle, his face literally devoured by pus: a kind of greenish filament in the bone of the forehead seemed to replace the path of a vein; he ate greedily the food that was offered to him, although remaining at a respectful distance; I thought I noticed on the front of his mantle a red triangle with the point at the top, and when he turned around I saw on his back a teardrop, an enormous embroidered teardrop which was as tall as he was; the point was at the top and it swelled out to the left:

and I immediately shrugged my shoulders at the image it
evoked in me; in fact, I made an effort to curb my always
hasty imagination; and yet I cannot deny the image that
presented itself to me at that moment; and I am going to
repeat this image at the risk of making you shrug your
shoulders as I did myself: I thought of the FIAT LUX of
God, and of the form which Robert Fludd, in his Théâtre
de l'Eternelle Sapience, uses to represent the original im-
pulse of the creation; this tear, this curved vessel—this
is how he represents the light which having emerged from
the void curves around gradually and surrounds the shadows which it is to replace; the tear alone might have
been nothing, but the red tear with the red triangle was
in itself a rather striking parallel; several weeks went by,
I penetrated the heart of the mountains, I saw the scattered priests of Peyote who grind all night on their rasps the
mixture of first principles; and I started on my way back.

I passed again through the village with the phallus and
on the stroke of noon asked for shelter at a wretched house
from which there emerged an Indian who in spite of the
torrid midday heat was enveloped in a huge mantle. I had
already seen some strange mantles in my travels over the
mountain: but this one had four extremely narrow white
triangles which occupied the entire length of the garment;
the borders were decorated with a line of crosses which

were green on one side and yellow on the other and were composed of the 4 triangles I have already mentioned; the Indian greeted us without a word, with a slow but intelligent smile; and already the woman was going to work. While she was preparing the corn and the greens I noticed a false braid that she wore attached to her hair; through this braid had been worked a length of yarn alternately green and yellow, the same colors as the crosses; and she also wore a necklace of green beads, and at her ears hung yellow stones; inside the house, children were fighting with shrill cries, and out came a very small boy with an enormous stomach, his mouth surrounded with boils, and behind him an older boy whom I recognized as the child in the gray mantle embroidered with a triangle and a teardrop; I saw nothing unusual inside the house except in one corner a cross whose top was a spearhead and whose arms were in the shape of trefoils. The Indian, when questioned, maintained a perfect silence.

There, dear friend, I wanted to tell you what I saw without drawing any sort of conclusion from it, you will see that the facts and the objects speak for themselves, and more convincingly no doubt than I have made them speak, although no doubt in the same sense. Perhaps someday I shall amuse myself by reporting, or I shall report without amusement, the world which all these things made me dream that I was entering, a world that I feel many modern things would gain a great deal by entering. It is not from the point of view of the picturesque that I wish to report this voyage but from the point of view of healing power.

Devotedly,   ANTONIN ARTAUD

I would have preferred you to tell me that it is the occult thesis itself that you do not like; and yet in all the obscurity that surrounds modern poetry and language there are far fewer ideas than in all this.

I am *very much* taken with this idea of the 3 Magi Kings which one finds at the source of several essential histories, and of a whole tradition. My essay is not overloaded; it is terribly concentrated and elliptical for the enormous subject which I have chosen to raise. But I am not done with this subject: I plan to bring it up again, in a different way, elsewhere; for the moment let's stick to this plan which you have proposed.

Very affectionately,

ANTONIN ARTAUD

To Jean Paulhan

[*February 27, 1937*]
Saturday

Dear friend,

I write you from the eye of a terrible storm, but one that is *necessary*. In a word, you have SAVED me.* I *know* now not only by intuition but by precise, I would even say mathematical, means of communication, that sensational things are about to happen, of which this ordeal was the first step.

Before coming here I had started to write the Peyote

---

* Jean Paulhan paid the bill for Artaud's stay on the rue Boileau. It is also very likely that he personally made the arrangements to have Artaud admitted to this establishment.—Gallimard ed.

Dance: it was impossible for me to finish it. And it is not until NOW that I begin to see what I wanted to say, which is so remote from what I was writing before I came here; ——— which is *myself*, in short, whereas the rest was only the caricature of myself, except for sudden flashes!!! Wasn't that letter full of things that I wrote you, at least fragments of it, one of these sudden flashes, and couldn't we append part of it to the Voyage? Especially the passage where I talk about the pustulous child. It seems to me we could.———

What do you think?

I won't ask you to write me: I'll come and see you after I leave here.

Affectionately,

ANTONIN ARTAUD

To Jean Paulhan

Saturday, March 13, 1937

Dear friend,

Here is one of the first things I have written since I left the Maison de Santé.

For a long time I have been wanting to do an article restating the question of astrology for our time. A communication which I mention in the article provided me with the occasion (For *l'air du mois?*) because it is of current interest.

I hope very much that you will be able to publish it in April.

You will see that it is a serious, documented article, and also one in which I think I have once again found my personal tone. I am also sending you the first part of the Peyote Dance under separate cover.

Affectionately,

ANTONIN ARTAUD

To Jean Paulhan

[Paris] March 28, 1937

Dear friend,

Here, AT LAST, is the final part of the Peyote Dance.

There is also a general conclusion, but I think that for the selection of Excerpts that is to appear in the *Revue,* this is enough. Since these are Excerpts from *A Voyage to the Land of the Tarahumara.*

Besides, the conclusion would excessively lengthen my text, which is already twice as long as *The Land of the Magi Kings,* which I have eliminated.

You now have all the pieces and you can make a decision.

All of the Peyote Dance has been *rewritten* in the spirit and feeling in which I revised, or rather in which I recast *The Mountain of Signs,* which you liked so much. I very much hope that this Dance as you now have it will please you as much. In any case, write me about it as soon as possible to set my mind at ease. But this time tell me *directly* what you think of it.

From my own point of view I have said in this Dance

exactly what I saw, and I have said it point by point. My personal impressions I have also described point by point. So there is no longer any arbitrary or preconceived thesis, no longer anything unfounded, but a mysterious thing in which what is visible is only the allusive outer garment, if you will, of something else infinitely more important, something *absolutely* important in itself. It seemed to me that this something was serious, was essential. And this will appear in my complete book on the voyage, about which I have *no doubt,* my dear Jean Paulhan, and I say this in all faith, in all conviction and sincerity, that it was guided by *the Invisible,* as I feel that my whole life is now guided. This is why I regard these Excerpts as an important Introduction to an event that will take place before long, as soon as I have fully recovered my forces on the deepest level, and why I am so anxious that it appear without too great a delay, before *the end of Spring,* in order to really be what it is, the groundwork for something else.

Forgive this enigmatic language.

You can't know how true it is and how grateful I am to you for serving by your two interventions* that which will come out of all this.

Affectionately,

ANTONIN ARTAUD

* In 1937, Jean Paulhan twice intervened successfully on Artaud's behalf: by supporting a request for assistance to the Writers' Fund (an emergency payment of 600 francs was granted by special arrangement on January 28, 1937); and by paying the expenses for Artaud's disintoxication treatment at the clinic on the rue Boileau. —Gallimard ed.

To Jean Paulhan

> Sceaux,
> April 13, 1937

Dear friend,

No news of you. I must confess that I am impatient to see the *Voyage* published at last. Didn't you receive my last long letter in which I give you all the details on the spirit in which *The Dance of Healing by Peyote* was written? I hope very much that you are completely satisfied with this text and that people will understand what I have tried to put into it—which is for me of absolute importance.

I received the proofs of *The Theater and Its Double*. I am very anxious that the preface be printed in italics. Anyway, I'm *rewriting it*. Couldn't you also find the other versions of certain texts which I had sent you by letter and which do not appear in the proofs that have been sent to me?

Until I see you, I am,

Yours very fondly,

ANTONIN ARTAUD

To Henri Parisot

> Rodez, December 10, 1943

Dear Sir,

I have written *Voyage to Mexico* of which the *Voyage to the Land of the Tarahumara* is the most important part. But the text of the *Voyage to the Land of the Tarahumara* is complete in itself. As for the *Voyage to Mexico*, it is a book of 200 pages or more which I worked on for eight months, from November 1936, the date of my return from Mexico, to August 1937, the date of my departure for Ireland, and which is not completely finished.

Merely in the time between September 1937 and today I have been arrested, put in prison in Dublin, deported to France, interned in Le Havre, transferred from Le Havre to Rouen, from Rouen to Sainte-Anne in Paris, from Sainte-Anne to Ville-Evrard, from Ville-Evrard to Chezal-Benoît and from Chezal-Benoît to Rodez. All my personal belongings have been confiscated by the police and all my papers have been lost. I have absolutely nothing left of what I possessed before, which consisted of a number of manuscripts, a billfold, and *above all* a little sword from Toledo 12 centimeters high with 3 fishhooks attached which was given to me by a Negro from Cuba. The director of the Prison of Dublin, Mr. de Soto, personally returned all my belongings to me. Even in Le Havre, where I was particularly badly treated, this sword was returned to me in the red leather case in which it was contained. At Sainte-Anne I still had my billfold, a brown alligator leather billfold with my initials, and the little red leather case containing the sacred sword, an object known to all Initiates, but since Ville-Evrard I no longer know what has become of these things. As for my personal papers and manuscripts, I have lost track of them since my return to France. And to rewrite this *Voyage to Mexico* and finish it would now take me almost a year. Besides, the atmosphere of confinement does not lend itself to this kind of work. In order to write, one must be free. Nevertheless, I am going to try to add a few pages to *A Voyage to the Land of the Tarahumara*. Dr. Ferdière, who is urging me strongly to do so, will see that I have all the facilities I need. In my six years of confinement he is the only doctor who has tried to mitigate my captivity within the limits of his means.

There is one thing of which I am certain, that it was at Chezal-Benoît that the little red leather case containing the sword from Toledo was not returned to me.

As for my manuscripts, it was when I was released from prison in Dublin that I saw them for the last time. After that I lost track of them.

Besides, we are all going through a period of trials and misfortunes and I cannot work when for the past three years I haven't had enough bread.

But, I repeat, I am going to make an effort to overcome all these obstacles and I will pray to Jesus Christ especially on this subject, for it is He who is behind my whole Voyage to Mexico and it is He, the Word of God, whom the Tarahumara worship, as I was able to observe in the Rite of *Tutuguri* which takes place exactly at the rising of the Sun.

And they themselves recognized this and told me so when two impressions of the Face of Christ were shown them. One on the Veil of Saint Veronica, the other on an Image taken at another moment of His Passion, and in which His True Face is perfectly recognizable. The sacerdotal class of the Indian Priests of the Sun regard themselves as a terrestrial emanation of his Virtue and his Force and each priest as the identification of one of his Rays. And one must see the wild energy with which each priest hurls himself to the ground at the precise moment when the solar hearth, which itself has never ceased to be free, is released in Indian consciousness from the imprisonment of the shadows of the night. One must see how each priest, by the position he knows how to take, reproduces with the other priests his brothers the extraordinary division of this hearth. But above all one must hear the Words which they send back and forth from one to the other with signs which seem drawn from the very edge of Eternity and which are made to sustain and manifest something, and this something is The Spirit of the Word which rolls like a ball of flame before the mouth of Lord God, and of which they, the Tara-Humara* remember, they say, having been and being the Will and the reflection.

But here they all began to weep, for as they told me: "This Will of God of which we were all the Angels, that is, the Rays, you see that very few of us still are, because too much Evil has passed over us. The war between Evil and God is not yet over and if the Kingdom of God is to come to earth we must be chaste. We are as chaste as possible. But people all over the earth are no longer chaste at all. And the time has come for them to return to complete chastity. For things were made by the sun and like him, and they were made like this," these priests told me, making certain signs with their arms and bodies which constitute the most extraordinary attitudes of Religious Dance I have ever seen.

Among these signs was the Sign of the Cross as the

---

* Written like this in the original letter. Artaud has broken *Tarahumara* into two elements: *Tara* suggests the famous historical, almost mythical site of Tara, in Ireland, with which Artaud was not unfamiliar; and *Humaras* the future of the verb *humer,* to inhale. One must also bear in mind the Sanskrit word *tara* meaning star, or the pupil of the eye.—Gallimard ed.

Catholics make it, but there was an infinity of other signs.

It is all this which I have already talked about in my manuscripts and which I am going to try to rewrite now. In the meantime, my warmest best wishes,

ANTONIN ARTAUD

Hôpital Psychiatrique,
1, rue Vieux-Sens,
Rodez,
Aveyron

P.S. Please give my best to Robert J. Godet, to whom all this is of particular interest.

Tutuguri: The Rite
of Black Night

*

Dedicated to the external glory of the sun *Tutuguri* is a
   black rite.
The Rite of black night and of the *eternal* death of the sun.
No, the sun will never come back
and the six crosses of the circle that the star must travel
   are really there only to bar its path.
For no one understands well enough, no one understands
   at all here in Europe that the cross is a black sign,
no one understands well enough *"the salivary power of the
   cross,"*
and that the cross is a stream of saliva spat on the words
   of thought.
In Mexico the cross and the sun are equals, and the leap-
   ing sun is this whirling phrase which takes six beats to
   reach the light of day,
the cross is a contemptible sign which must be burned by
   matter,
why contemptible,
because the tongue which salivates its sign is contemptible,

and why does it salivate its sign?

To anoint it.

For no sign is holy or sacred unless it is anointed.

But at the moment the tongue anoints it does it not form a point?

does it not place itself between the four cardinal points?

So when the sun appears it must leap over the six points of the contemptible phrase to be saved, of which it will make a kind of translation on the level of lightning.

For the sun really appears at the height of the crosses like a ball of lightning,

and one knows that it will not forgive.

It will not forgive what?

The sin of man and of the surrounding village,

and this is why several weeks before the rite you can see the entire race of the Tarahumara purging themselves, washing, and dressing in clean white garments.

And the Day of the Rite and of the blinding apparition has finally arrived.

And now they are made to lie on the ground in their white garments, the six men regarded as the purest of the tribe.

And each is thought to have married a cross.

One of those crosses made of two sticks tied together with a dirty cord.

And there is a seventh man who stands with a cross tied to his hip, and in his hands is a bizarre musical instrument made of many slats of wood laid one on top of the other,

and the slats make a sound between a bell and a gun.

And on a certain day, at dawn, the seventh Tutuguri opens
the dance by striking one of the slats with a deep black
iron mallet.

Then you see the men with the crosses, who have sprung
up as if out of the ground, leap forward in a circle, and
each must go around his cross seven times without
breaking the whole circle.

I do not know whether it is because the wind is rising,

or whether a wind rises from this music of another time
which is still alive today,

but one feels as if lashed by a gust of night, by a breath
that has risen from the burial vaults of a dead race that
has come to show its face here,

a painted face,

a face mocking and without mercy.

Without mercy because the justice that it brings is not of
this world.

Be pure and chaste,

it seems to say.

Be virginal too.

Or I will show you my Gehenna.

And Gehenna opens.

The wood harp of the seventh Tutuguri is now throbbing
horribly: it is the crater of a volcano at the height of its
eruption.

The slats seem to be breaking beneath the sounds like a
forest blasted by the ax of a fantastic woodcutter.

And suddenly what one was waiting for happens:

sulphurous fumes, *lilac-laden*, emerge in a mass from a
point in the circle

which the six men

                    have traced,
which the six crosses
                    have enclosed,
and from beneath the fumes a flame, an enormous flame
                    suddenly
flashes,
and this enormous flame *boils*.
It boils with an *unearthly* sound. Its interior is filled with
    stars, with incandescent bodies; as if the sun in coming
    brought with it a celestial system.
And behold, the sun has taken its position.
It has formed in the middle of a celestial system. It has
    suddenly placed itself as if at the center of a tremendous
    explosion.
For the flaming bodies like the soldiers of an army at war
    have fallen on each other, bursting.
Now the sun has become round. And one can see a ball of
    flame on the same axis as the natural sun rise and leap
    from cross to cross, for it is dawn.
The six men have opened their arms, not in the form of a
    cross, but with their hands forward, as if trying to catch
    the ball, and the ball, turning around each planted cross,
    endlessly escapes.
For the wood harp is a wind, it has become like the floor of
    a wind over which an army could advance.
And so it does.
Now at the confines of the sound and of the void, for the
    sound is so loud
That it calls forth nothing
but the void,
there is a violent stamping. The measured rhythm of an

army on the march, or the galloping hoofs of a stam-
pede.
The flaming ball has burned the six crosses; the six men
with their hands held out who have seen the thing come
are all six
                    exhausted and amazed.
And the sound of galloping hoofs grows louder.
And on the horizon of crosses one sees a shape like a run-
away horse coming closer
with a naked man on top
for the beat of the rhythm was 7.
But there are only six crosses.
And in the wood harp of the seventh Tutuguri
always a beginning of nothingness
always this beginning of nothingness:
this empty beat,
an empty beat,
a kind of exhausting void between the slats of sharp wood,
a void calling the trunk of man,
the sawed-off torso of man
into the furor (not into the fervor)
of the things within.
There, where underneath the void
                    are chosen
the sound of great bells in the wind,
the rending of naval cannons,
the baying of waves in the tempests of the south;
there, the advancing horse bears the torso of a man,
a naked man who holds aloft
not a cross,
but a staff of ironwood,

attached to a giant horseshoe
that encircles his whole body,
his body cut with a slash of blood,
and the horseshoe is there
like the jaws of an iron collar
which the man has caught
in the slash of his blood.

Ivry-sur-Seine, February 16, 1948

(*continued from front flap*)

world of Europe is losing . . . I felt
therefore that I should go back to the
source and expand my pre-conscious
to the point where I could see myself
evolve and *desire*. And Peyote led me
to this point."

The Peyote Dance is the story of
Artaud's visit to the Tarahumara, re-
fracted through his varying states of
mind and transcribed over and over—
each time illuminating another aspect
of his art and his obsessive attempts
to expand the pre-conscious.

Jacket design by Bob Korn